THE POWER
OF
FEMININITY

Michelle McKinney
HAMMOND

HARVEST HOUSE PUBLISHERS
Eugene, Oregon 97402

Cover by Koechel Peterson & Associates, Minneapolis, Minnesota

THE POWER OF FEMININITY

Copyright © 1999 by Michelle McKinney Hammond
Published by Harvest House Publishers
Eugene, Oregon 97402

Library of Congress Cataloging-in-Publication Data

McKinney Hammond, Michelle, 1957–
      The power of femininity / Michelle McKinney Hammond.
         p.   cm.
      ISBN 0-7369-0142-6
      1. Christian women—Religious life.   2. Christian women—Conduct of life.
   3. Femininity—Religious aspects—Christianity.   4. Man-woman relationships—
   Religious aspects—Christianity.   I. Title.
   BV4527.M42   1999
   248.8'43—DC21   99-24433
                                                                                                  CIP

Dedication

To my mother,
Norma McKinney,
who taught me to rejoice in being a woman by example.

*Not only did you fill my life with all the wonders of
femininity, but you gave me the precious gift
of sharing my life with many mothers.*

The women in my family are
each extraordinary women in their
own right. They have reflected the beauty, the grace,
and the triumph of the feminine spirit to me,
a little girl who watched them all in wonder.
I pray that I have become
a composite of the best parts of them all.

Alexandra Petrona Branker
Sarah Ayodele Sam
Charity Hammond
Eglantine White
Ernesta Forde
Marion Arkaah
Rosamond Aba Hammond

I love you all.

Acknowledgments

To the Harvest House family: Thank you for laboring with me.
Bob Hawkins, Jr., Bill Jensen, Steve Miller—I appreciate you more
than words can say. Carolyn McCready, Betty Fletcher, LaRae Weikert,
Janna Walkup, Julie McKinney, Teresa Evenson, Hope Lyda,
Trina Marshall, Ruth Samsel, Jennifer Wellette—
you are living examples of exactly what I'm talking about.
You have made me celebrate sisterhood all the more!
Thank you for making my work so enjoyable.

Nicole, thank you for being my right arm.
You are such a great sister, I love you so much!

Sheila, thanks for keeping me straight, girl.
Bunny and Terri, keep nudging and pushing me.
Peggy, keep cheering.
Diane, keep interceding.
Cindy, keep listening.
Charlotte, Jan, Karen, Michelle,
Brenda, Theresa, and Dee Dee—you know what to do.
What women!

Ian and Okuru, Nanapiah—
every woman should have brothers as protective
and loveable as you.

Daryll, Jeff, Joel, and Tony—
my precious buds...
What can I say? Thanks for affirming that being a for-real woman
is a good thing!

Contents

A Note from the Author

Relationships between men and women—both platonic and romantic—are in trouble. It is as if all the actors in the play of love have forgotten their lines and staging directions. What was supposed to be a classic romance has turned into a tragedy with all of the players doing nothing more than stepping on one another's toes and limping offstage to their respective dressing rooms. The audience is left confused, while the actors themselves are befuddled as to what really happened.

The popular theater line, "There are no small parts, only small actors," seems appropriate here. Men and women are different and were created so deliberately by God. Yet present-day moral issues and the fight for equal rights have left most men and women confused about who they are, where they fit, and what they mean to one another. Women have felt devalued and powerless. This causes them to embrace the modern-day opinion that they must operate by male standards in order to gain respect in the world. But the real tragedy is that the transition back to being a soft woman after leaving the hardness of the boardroom becomes more and more difficult. It is safe to say many have lost their way back to femininity.

Oh, the backlash this creates in male/female relationships! The anxiety it causes in the spirits of women who can't quite put their finger on what is wrong! It's truly overwhelming. *The Power of Femininity* is a journey back to the basics to reclaim the pieces of self that countless women have lost in the struggle to validate their own sense of worth.

Through biblical insights in light of modern-day illustrations, God's original design for woman will be explored, thus supplying a map "back to the garden," so to speak. It is my prayer that this book will liberate, heal, and release women to celebrate who they were created to be and discover the true source of their value and power.

ONE

Woman to Woman

Somewhere between her home
         and a placard demanding equal rights
              she got lost
              wandering past the garden
                   following where the serpent pointed
                        she turned left instead of right
                             and got offtrack...
and though the scenery looked vaguely familiar
         a frown of consternation
              began to crease her brow
                   as she realized
                        it was taking her
                             far too long
                                  to reach her desired destination
              still she determined to go
                   yet another mile
                        before turning off her chosen path
                             perhaps she was being too anxious...
and as she wandered
         looking for a marker
              to get her bearings
         man wondered where she'd gone
              as she ventured too far to hear
                        his need for her
                   or her children crying
         and they too lost their way
              trying to follow her
         misled by traces of her perfume in the air
              the memory of a gentle touch
                   an encouraging word...
              a piece of fabric soft to the skin

and sage advice
   were found along the path
  now littered with confusion
   and distrust...
and as man's shoulders began to slope in resignation
    weakening his arms
     causing him to abdicate his seat as protector
   and her children began to find their own way
   allowing new friends of rebellion
    to fill the space she left behind
    a cry rang out...
  it filled the earth
   it reached the skies
   and rang throughout the heavens
"Woman, where art thou?"
"Woman, where art thou?"
"Woman, where art thou?"
  it echoed off the mountaintops
  and stretched across the plains
   it descended throughout the valleys
   this plaintive cry
  mourning the absence
   of this precious lost treasure
and she hearing the cry
  came to a halt
   not quite sure of where she stood
unable to give her location
  she turned looking for her own
   footprints in the sand
  only to find shallow remembrances
  of where she had been

and somewhere between her struggle to recall her true identity
    and the place of her restoration
        she saw visions of a man with sad eyes
            longing for her love
                praying for her return
        and children
            with their arms outstretched
                crying for her wisdom to save them
                        but she had grown weary from the journey...
    sadness rooting her to the spot
        depression bowing her
            into herself
        she succumbed to her fatigue
                sinking into a deep and fitful sleep...
        and in the distance
                the ring of hammers
                            began hesitantly
                building
                    and building again
                until it reverberated
            through the land...
        its sharp rhythm piercing the hearts of men
        awakening sleeping women
            and frustrated children
    as wanted signs were posted
            by determined hands
                    in search of the vanishing woman...

$\mathcal{L}$adies, can we talk? Talk about why women are frustrated and men are confused? Talk about where we lost our way and what that really means? Talk about where all the good men have gone and why so many are wandering? Let's talk about the fine print we've neglected to read and how much that oversight has cost us. About the power that we've thrown to the wind. About what's happening to our relationships. Our children. Our hearts. Our souls. Let's talk about how the art of being a woman has become a near-extinct and priceless treasure. And how those who stumble across it treat it as an antique they don't know the value of—tossing it aside, preferring the newer, more streamlined, cheaper model of so-called liberation. Funny how you never realize the value of Grandma's brass bed until you get older and find out how much others are willing to pay for what we so easily discard.

As creation longs for the original plan of peaceful coexistence, the groans of weary women have come before the throne of God. The vicious cycle of men abdicating, women rising up, men fleeing, and women becoming embittered, hardened, and hopeless has tainted society and caused wonderment in the heavens. The lines are invisibly drawn, silently proclaiming war. Romance lies trampled underfoot and understanding lies shattered beneath hurled insults and accusations.

Ladies, can we talk? I mean talk without pretense, posturing, or qualifying. After all, real life is not a talk show. I often wonder if anyone is really tuned in to real life. I wonder if anyone is really seeing what we're doing to one another. How we're robbing one another. Hurting one another. Killing one another. The golden rule of "love your neighbor as you love yourself" has been broken, snapped over the knees of those determined to seize what they want in blind frustration with total disregard for the whole picture. Can we talk about getting off the merry-go-round? Can we talk woman-to-woman about how we've "lost it" and how to get "it" back?

Can we talk about calling a truce with one another—with our men—and finding ourselves again? Let's talk about acknowledging and learning to celebrate this simple fact— men and women are different. I long for all women to sink back into the glorious place of truly being women in the same way I long for a hot bath when all of my muscles are screaming. The warmth of the water closes over my limbs like a liquid blanket, wrapping itself around me, becoming intimate with every part of me. I do not recoil from this. Rather, I embrace it because it sets me free from pain, free from the struggle I've endured all day long. It defies my further efforts to stay afloat all by myself in the world. It gently invites me to let go. Let go of all I think I should be. Let go of the demands of others. Let go and just be. Just be a woman. Naked and unashamed. Warm and soft. Content in my liquid cocoon. Relaxed and unthreatened. Just a woman—lost in the oasis of being me. Ladies, can we talk—I mean *really* talk—about where we went wrong? Can we talk without shouting?

"I am woman, hear me roar...." Well, I don't know about you, but I don't want to roar or go to war! I believe I can speak in a normal tone and still be heard. That I can stand perfectly still and manage to get things done. That I can influence rather than provoke, inspire rather than challenge. That I can affect a nation from my home. That I can move mountains with my faith. Why? Because God said so! Yes, girlfriend, it's time to get this thing right, not just for the sake of your own joy level but also for the peaceful state of that which emanates from your own personal kingdom. Your home, your job, your church, your community, your city, your state, your nation. Your stake in eternity. Your investment in God's economy. You see, for every action you can expect a reaction, like a pebble in a pond that ripples far beyond you. So pull up a chair and sit down, honeychile; it's time to talk—woman-to-woman.

Dear Heavenly Father, there are so many voices with various expectations filling my world. Sometimes I find myself confused and even frustrated in my search to establish who I really am. Help me to remember that You hold the key to my true identity. You created me to be a valuable addition to mankind and a living expression and example of Your heart. Blot out the lies the enemy tries to plant in my soul to devalue me. As I cling to the truth from Your Word that tells me I am "fearfully and wonderfully made" a woman on purpose, let the revelation of what that truly means saturate my being, releasing me to celebrate my womanhood, and to rejoice in the gift I am to the world. Help me to resonate with a sense of divine purpose. Grant me the confidence to walk in Your original design for my life. Restore to me the gift of my femininity and help me to harbor it as a treasure in my heart. As I release it like a heady perfume from the inner sanctum of my spirit, use it to heal others around me as I touch them with my special brand of softness. And I will always be mindful to give the glory back to You as You exhibit Your love through my arms to liberate others to be all You created them to be, in Jesus' name. Amen.

TWO

Back to Basics

$\mathcal{L}$ike a phoenix rising
she rose in slow motion
with the earth reluctant
to release her
pungent with its
musky scent
soft and molded
resembling earth
with its mountains
and its valleys
crests and peaks
she rose
silently
hesitantly
gaining her footing
steadying herself on
long slim legs
that were yet unsure
of standing...
she rose and stood
breathing in the air
God had breathed into her
feeling her soul unfold its wings within her...
the early dusk
reflected highlights of deep amber
red
and golden brown
upon her skin
as the earth from which she had been formed
damp and moist
still clung insistently

to her limbs
she rose
she stood
she waited...
waited until *he* arose
this man
this setting from which she had been taken
even now she felt the phantom remains
of other ribs encircling her
making her feel safe
as she awaited her discovery...
bone of his bone
flesh of his flesh
yet a separate entity
she breathed in harmony with him
feeling his pulse
hearing his heartbeat in her head
she was one with him
though outside of him
and when he awoke he knew
instinctively
profoundly
and definitely knew
that this was woman
a mirror of himself
the extension of his own arms
and so he wrapped himself around her
tucking her beneath his heart
to keep her warm
and the two became one
balancing the weight of life between them

and in the face of every tempest
        she arose
                in his strength which had become hers
        and hers his
        she arose to redefine him daily
        as a glorious testament
                of all that was beautiful
                        all that was pure
                                and all that was good
                        she arose to embrace the origin
                                of who she was
                who she would always be
                        woman
                        taken from man
                        from the earth
                        the signature of God
        completing the sentence that man had begun
        bringing him to life
                carrying the breath of His spirit within her...
        the glory of her man
                the covering of her children
        the giver of life
she could not be contained
        for she bore all things within herself
                and in this capacity
                        she arose to give
                                as only a woman can give
                for it is a gift to the world
                        this creation called woman...

*A*nd so Eve stretched in the morning sun, carefully studying Adam, tracing the place beneath his rib from where God had taken her. He was something for her to behold, as she was something to see to him. He was soft, yet strong. He was like her, yet different. His voice was deep and resonant in her ears, different from all the other sounds her ears were growing accustomed to in the garden. His voice, in comparison to the sounds of the creatures surrounding them, produced a unique reaction within her. It caused a fluttering deep in the pit of her stomach. When he touched her skin, she felt a warmth flush through her entire being that magnified the coolness of the wind. She felt safe in his nearness. And how he cared for her! From the moment he saw her, he never ceased to make her feel cherished. He reveled in her beauty, celebrated her gentility, and gloried in her wonder of him. In the midst of their paradise, he taught her things, of creation and of God.

To Adam, Eve was a wonder to consider—the most incredible of all God's creations. She was so soft, so warm. So comforting and nurturing and giving. She made him feel like a king. All he wanted to do was protect her and give her every-thing her heart desired. Her voice caressed him, her touch created feelings in him that were indescribable, and she had the most interesting way of looking at things! She reintro-duced him to wonders that had grown commonplace in their familiarity. How could he have overlooked them before? She was right! The colors in a butterfly's wings were unlike any other hue. Often he found himself standing in silent obser-vance of her, watching the way she moved, the tilt of her head when she listened to a bird sing. The sound of her laughter was music to him, and he wondered how he had ever existed without her. Breathing thanks to God for such a marvelous gift he rejoined his beautiful wife. He wished to find out what the serpent had said to her that was so intriguing.

The Contest Begins

"Oh, don't be silly," the serpent said. "He's just afraid you will be like Him." Was he talking about Adam, or God? It's an important question. Because many things in the spiritual world are parallel to things in the natural world, I believe the serpent was speaking of both. He planted his seed well. The fight for "equal rights" began that day in the garden, dis-rupting the peaceful coexistence between man and woman—and between man, woman, and God—forevermore. "'For God knows that when you eat of [the fruit] your eyes will be opened, and you will be like God, knowing good and evil.'" (Genesis 3:5 NIV). *Being like God*—a powerful image in the mind of one so innocent. To know everything and to be lord over one's own destiny had to be good things, weren't they? Although Eve didn't dare consider the thought of being equal to God, the fruit was looking more and more delicious by the minute as she considered the serpent's words. His voice was so hypnotic, she felt as if she were standing outside of herself, hearing his words from a distance. The color of the fruit was so rich. It appeared to have so much more substance than the rest of the diverse fruits from which she could eat freely of in the garden. This fruit was special, indeed; she could just imagine how wonderful it tasted. The serpent's point made sense—it could never hurt to gain more wisdom. Perhaps he was right. Perhaps she had misinterpreted what God had said.

And so she ate. And she shared it with Adam. And he, too, ate. But the result was not what they had anticipated. All of a sudden she felt strange. Why was Adam looking at her that way? Why did he recoil when she looked at him? She looked down and gasped, taking a step back in horror. Why hadn't she realized it before? She was naked! Suddenly she was not as beautiful as she had originally thought, and in her shame she sought to cover herself. Adam, too, frantically devised a way to shield himself from Eve's prying eyes. But the way he felt beneath her scrutiny was nothing compared to the wave of dread that overtook him as he heard the Lord approaching. He sucked in his breath as Eve's eyes widened at the sound of the Lord's voice calling them, and they silently hid themselves. "Where are you?" the Lord said. Why would He ask such a question? He had never asked them that before. He always used to know exactly where they were. They'd never hidden before. Why was everything changing?

It was such an unsettling feeling. A foreboding that the worst was yet to come hung like a wet, impenetrable curtain in the atmosphere. Suddenly the air was thick and humid, and Adam was having a hard time breathing. Finally he cleared his throat and decided to bite the bullet. Stepping forward, he decided that a simple explanation would do. "Oh, we heard You. We just didn't think we should offend You by greeting You in our nakedness." "Who told you that you were naked?" the Lord said. Adam felt trapped by his own admission. He had not anticipated this question. He didn't quite know how to answer without showing his entire hand. But God knew and gently confronted him, "Have you eaten from the tree I told you not to eat from?" This was man's first opportunity to own up to his sin and repent, but, no—Adam's shame made it impossible for him to speak the truth. So he transferred the blame to Eve. Perhaps God would go easy on them and grant them a measure of grace if she took the brunt of the blame. After all, she had just come on the scene; she didn't fully know the ropes yet. So Adam said, "It was 'that woman' (sound familiar?) whom *You* gave me." You can well imagine the rest of what he wanted to say: "I didn't ask for her, remember; You gave her to me. You know You never had any trouble with me until she came along. Surely You know I didn't think this up on my own." So Adam blamed God and Eve blamed the serpent, and the serpent just hunched his shoulders and said, "Hey, if You hadn't kicked me out of heaven, none of this would have happened." And all three received a punishment in keeping with their crime.

Because of woman's deception, some things in the garden were about to change. From this day forward, she would feel the pain of childbirth, a pain that she had caused God to feel when she wrenched herself from His protective womb to become master of her own destiny. Because the scripture in Genesis 3:16 is so often used in the "submission" debate, I would like to shed further light on this curse that affected all women. This scripture is not about position or submission. If that were the case, single women would have been exempt from the curse. This scripture is about the state of the fallen heart, which we will take a deeper look at later in the book. No one's position in the garden changed it. Man was responsible for covering and leading woman from the beginning. But now any woman, married or single, would find herself always striving to have man bend to her will. She would seek to grasp total fulfillment from man, to receive complete affirmation from him, but she would never achieve this fulfillment because no human being could be her completion. In other words, the curse caused the heart of woman to say to man, "I need you to be willing to do anything for me, including disobeying God if that's what it takes to make me feel loved, desired, worthy, and fulfilled." The fall caused the God-given *desire* in her heart for man to be perverted into a *need* for him for all the wrong reasons. Man could never live up to the void the fall created, so woman's exaggerated need for man became her bondage. Her desire for him would now "rule" over her and color all of her decisions as she constantly strove to gain his love in a spot reserved for God alone.

On the other hand, though God created them as partners, Adam had been there first. He knew all the rules. Adam's assignment was to have dominion over *every living thing*. He was to lovingly administer order and direction. This made him responsible for taking care of Eve. You know the oldest child syndrome. Therefore, in God's eyes Adam abdicated his role as protector of Eve, listening to her wrongful suggestion when he knew better. Because he chose to willfully follow her into disobedience, he would now get to see how it felt to have the object of his affection rebel against him. In addition, he would be destined to struggle for all of his life with that which had once been simple. As for Satan, he would be at war with woman and her offspring, striking out to destroy her and the seed of her womb at every turn, yet never gaining the victory because he was cursed evermore, destined to be ultimately defeated by Christ Himself.

The Little Green Lie

"Who told you that you were naked?" This is where it all began. The question that opened the door to the little lie that became an even bigger fabrication over the course of time. Who told you to be ashamed of who you are, woman? Who told you that womanhood has no worth? Who told you that the device God put in place to protect woman was evidence that she was unworthy of being acknowledged for her priceless value? Who told you that embracing your femininity was a losing proposition? Who told you that it's a man's world? A world where women should just take a backseat and accept their second-class citizenship in life? Certainly these words never came from God's lips. And if God didn't say them, they have no grounds to stand up in court. Yet Satan planted this one little seed, one itty-bitty lie. Behold, how great a tree can grow from one tiny seed, bearing a crop of fruit most poisonous.

And so began woman's suspicion that man was keeping something behind his back that he didn't want her to have. How dare he not want us to be like him! Who died and appointed him king, anyway? And why didn't God want us to be like Him and know good and evil? First of all, God never said that. It was His intent that we would be His sons and daughters, that we would be like Him because we would walk in perfect fellowship with Him, seeing Him as He is (1 John 3:2). It was never His intent for us to be *like* Him *apart* from Him. This would be too dangerous, for we would self-destruct. Why? Because we are not God. We are created beings. Created in His image, now able to discern good from evil like Him, but still different from God. He created Himself in His own omniscience, omnipotence, omnipresence, and unlimitedness. We are none of the above in our earthly state. Yet so great is the love that He lavishes on us that He set boundaries in order to keep us from hurting ourselves. I once heard a preacher say, "God's Word isn't all that He knows; it's all that He knows we can handle." He knew that to add any more than what He had already deposited in man would only corrupt and destroy an earthly vessel. But even in the midst of these sublimely perfect conditions, something in woman caused her to reach for the stove like an inquisitive child and burn her hands.

What happened? How did we ever go from the garden to the war zone? I believe it is necessary to retrace our steps in order to find where we took a wrong turn. Let's start back at the beginning, where there was God, creation, and man. Everything was cool. Everybody was happy. Everybody got along. Then God had a brilliant idea! (Most of the time I think it was brilliant, anyway.) He decided that it wasn't good for man to be alone. Poor thing, this creature needed help. God had given him a lot of work to do, and He realized that Adam needed help staying focused on it. He would need extra encouragement from time to time. He needed someone to fill in the blanks, take up the slack, keep him together. He needed a "helpmeet," a partner—someone designed especially to complement him in every way. This person would add dimension to his life, would be strong where he was weak. This person, called woman, would assist him in completing his assignment to subdue, maintain order, cultivate, and take care of God's creation, to be fruitful and multiply. These things he could not do without her help. He didn't realize he needed anything outside of himself, but he would...soon. Sometimes you don't know what you're missing until it is right in front of you.

In the Beginning

And so God set to work fashioning Eve from Adam. He stood back after breathing the breath of life into her and admired His handiwork, "Oh, this is good!" He exclaimed. She was fearfully and wonderfully made. In the words of Matthew Henry, "If man is the head, she (woman) is the crown, a crown to her husband, the crown of the visible creation. The man was dust refined, but the woman was double-refined, one remove further from the earth....The woman was made of a rib out of the side of Adam; not made out of his head to rule over him, nor out of his feet to be trampled upon by him, but out of his side to be equal with him, under his arm to be protected, and near his heart to be beloved." Ah, doesn't that sound wonderful? And so it was in the beginning, until that ole serpent showed up.

The serpent was slick and calculating. He knew some things that Eve had yet to realize. First of all, he knew of God's plan for man, and it didn't sit well with him. He refused to stand by and watch man become like God after his own plan to be like God had failed so miserably. He knew from experience that rebellion was the one thing which God would not allow in His presence. He had to cause a breach in Adam and Eve's relationship with God. Then they would never attain the status he himself had so deeply longed for. Secondly, the serpent knew never to underestimate the power of woman. He knew the effect she had on man. This is why she became his target. He realized that the best way to pull man down was through the woman. One look from her could sink ships. One word of praise could cause him to leap tall buildings in a single bound. One disparaging comment would incapacitate him better than a collision with a Mack truck. Yes, the woman was definitely the best way to defeat the man and foil God's plan.

The serpent knew something else. He knew that if he could cause man and woman to reach for a mirage, they would lose their footing and fall. And so he influenced them to release what they already had in order to go for the golden ring, knowing they would miss it completely. Think of it. Adam and Eve were created in God's image, eternal spirits with souls inhabiting bodies, reflecting the three facets of the Trinity—the Holy Spirit, God, and Jesus—yet made manifest in bodily form. They were living souls, walking in dominion and sinless. Though they were not God, they were as close to His likeness as they could be in their humanness. What else was there for them to desire? The only thing that would work was a lie. But because to the pure everything is pure, it probably never occurred to Eve that he was telling a lie. The serpent knew what Eve didn't yet realize, that her identity or "God-likeness" was wrapped up in God Himself. He had to get her to bid for being "lord of her own destiny" before she found out he was trying to sell her an empty box. You see, God does not feel the necessity to experience evil in order to know it is evil. God discerns evil and avoids it. That is what He longs for us to do. But Adam and Eve took their lives into their own hands, ate from the tree of knowledge of good and evil, and lost their "God-like" status.

When Seeing Costs More Than Believing

Instead of finding themselves like God, Adam and Eve found the only thing they really knew was that they were now ashamed of their nakedness. Eve found out something else that was very interesting. She found out that when man was ashamed, he became insecure. And when he became insecure, he became defensive and cast blame upon her. She became the enemy in the midst of his shame and failure.

Failure was a weight that Adam could not bear. It emasculated him in the presence of Eve. And as a man whose heart had been made in the image of his Creator, longing for worship and praise, he knew he had forfeited that which was so important to him the moment he fell for the lie of the serpent. And because he submitted to the woman's hand that held the fruit, he would now have to struggle for her respect and submission for the rest of his days. Wasn't this all just too ironic?

Although the serpent was also cursed, he was satisfied that the first phase of his mission had been accomplished. He had successfully caused man to forfeit his God-ordained authority upon the earth, severed the relationship between man and God, and drew battle lines between man and woman. Now he always would have the woman as an open door to get at the man, using her power of influence, her charms, her tongue, and her body to penetrate the man's exterior. And he would use the man against the woman to cast blame and inflict authority rather than inspire submission. He would use man's confusion to victimize that which he should protect. These factors, once put in place, would guarantee unending friction between the two genders for generations to come. Perhaps it would even destroy the family unit as God had planned it, and wouldn't that be grand?

Bump up this scenario to the present day and we all stand as witnesses to the damage done in the garden. We now have resorted to considering the idea that "men are from Mars and women are from Venus" in order to explain our differences. But the truth of the matter is, no matter how clever the cliché, we are not from different planets. Our origin is much closer than either of us can readily conceive. We are part of one another with visible and invisible differences. We were made to benefit, not be at odds with, one another. Understanding and celebrating our differences instead of blaming and bashing is the first step we must take.

We women lost it when we failed to recognize our own unique power. Instead we got locked into a power struggle that never existed from God's vantage point.

Where True Power Lies

I submit to you that we women have lost our hallowed position by trying to assimilate into what we consider to be a male world. Now before you get all excited, I would like you to hear me out. God did not design a man's world. God's design for the world was man and woman working together in peaceful harmony, building one another up and promoting each other to good works—namely our God-given assignments on the earth—that others would observe the fruits of our lives and give glory to God.

We women lost it when we failed to recognize our own unique power. Instead we got locked into a power struggle that never existed from God's vantage point. Struggling to get the credit for something I still can't figure out, we put man on the defensive. And that put us on the defensive. Now, with everyone defending themselves, we are all losing ground.

It is time to take off the boxing gloves and allow God to redistribute His first commission to us—man and woman both in power because of their status as complementary partners. This is what I would like us to consider together. The world has definite ideas about what power looks like, but God's view of power is very different. For example, He says that "the meek shall inherit the earth" (Psalm 37:11 KJV). Meekness is actually strength under control, strength that keeps its cool and doesn't show out. As women who have chosen to walk in the spiritual dimension, it behooves us to understand kingdom principles in the light of who we are and who we were meant to be as women. We will take a slow and leisurely walk through the list in this very book as we seek to find direction for mending our relationships with ourselves, with one another, and with men as we recover God's initial design for us.

Let's get back to Eve and take a closer look at how this whole mess evolved, shall we? Think about why she was created in the first place. God said that it wasn't good for man to be alone. God said that man needed a "helpmeet," in other words, a helper who would be equipped to help him in the manner in which he needed help. *God* said it; *Adam* didn't say it. This is important to note. Man did not realize that he needed help. In fact, man still does not know that he needs help! This is confirmed every time a man refuses to ask for directions when he gets lost. You know what I'm talking about! So the number one fact here that we need to remember in order to start feeling valuable and powerful is that *man needs help.*

Now, this doesn't mean that you need to tell him that. This is privileged information given in order for you to understand your power source. Man does not do well without woman. God has given each of us specific gifts in order to equip us to be a specific man's helper. Your gifts may differ from that of another sister, and that's fine because she was created to assist a different type of man. This is why you must understand up front that not just any man will do for you, or vice versa. It is important to partner with the person God has designed you to assist. And vice versa. This is important to the fulfillment of you both. This is why being aware of your own personal purpose and areas of gifting is essential before partnering. How else will you know if your marriage will be a good partnership? How will he know that you are the one whom he needs to assist him? How will you know that he's the one who can make the most out of your gifts?

Examining Your Gifts

So what exactly do you bring to the party? Well, let's see...influence for one thing. While man has been given the mandate of authority, woman has been given the mantle of influence. Quiet as it's kept, influence is more powerful than authority. Surprised? Stay tuned...we will explore this concept more indepth later. In the meantime, until you get a deeper understanding, never underestimate your power of influence. With little or no effort, you can get your man to do things no one else can. It is a function of your simply being who you are. Besides influence, you also have intuition—the ability to be spiritually sensitive, to read the fine print in a given situation. And how could I forget this next one? It's a biggie. Your sexuality and your reproductive abilities. You have something that every man wants. You possess the ability to make him feel better than any successful business merger or football game could ever make him feel. Plus you hold the power to lengthen his days through producing generations that bear his name. That is powerful. It's too powerful a gift to be abused or misused. Now, this gift list gives you a whole lot to work with and it should negate the need to resort to masculine tactics to get your heart's desire without experiencing a boomerang effect.

Let's go ahead with further exploration of the basic plan. God says that man is the image and glory of God. "But the woman is the glory of man" (1 Corinthians 11:7 NIV).

Well, what exactly does that mean? What exactly is glory? Glory is the presence, the power, the supremacy of God made manifest upon the earth. Man is the mirror reflection of God, made in His image. He is an eternal soul with a mind, a will, and emotions like the Godhead. Man is a complete representation of the Triune God, the Three-in-One. Remember that in the garden, God, Jesus, and the Holy Spirit conferred together, and yet the scripture says, "And God said, Let us make man in our image, after our likeness" (Genesis 1:26 KJV, emphasis added).

Isn't that awesome? God is so vast in all of His attributes that they could not all be contained in one part, yet He chose to combine His infinite qualities to dwell in the encasement of finite man, as in *mankind*. Therefore, the woman also shares in this commission because she came out of the man. She is one with the man. She is man with a womb. I believe that while man and woman were both created in the image of God, each was uniquely created to emphasize specific parts of God's nature, with man leaning more toward the mind of God, and woman toward the heart of God. Together, they complement one another in such a way as to reflect God in His totality. "So God created man in his own image, in the image of God created he him; male and female created he them" (Genesis 1:27 KJV). We could spend quite a bit of time meditating on this, but let's continue.

There is an order to this intricate design. Just as Jesus is also God and wields great authority yet yields to the direction of the Father, so is woman called to yield to the direction of the man. This is not a forfeiture but rather a continuance of the authority structure that God put in place. Just as every knee will bow and every tongue confess that Jesus is Lord to the glory of God the Father, this glory thing was designed to have a ripple effect. The woman then represents the presence, the strength, and the authority of the man upon the earth. I am not talking about abuses of power; I am addressing the basic plan of God's design before Satan began to pervert relationships between the sexes. Think of it this way. When I was a child and my father was not currently present at home, my mother became the reigning authority who preserved order on the home front. She represented my father. To usurp her authority was to earn the resounding message, "Wait until your father gets home!" And you knew, as your heart sank to the floor, that now you were really in trouble. Time taught you to just be smart and do as Mother said. Get the picture?

In the earth, as well as in a household, order is established when both reigning parties walk in agreement. "And if a house be divided against itself, that house cannot stand" (Mark 3:25 KJV). And so it is in marriage and family relationships. Children will always test each parent to find the weak link. Pitting authority against authority, they see which parent will be the one they can ultimately manipulate in order to get their way. And so Satan pits man against woman and woman against man, all in the name of "equal rights," "liberation," and "having your own way." The goal is to make a laughingstock of us all as we careen down the pathway of destroyed marriages and confused relationships, crashing and burning in a bitter heap of frustration and hopelessness.

Remember, Eve *influenced* Adam to eat of the fruit. Herein lies our first lesson. She didn't grow hair on her chest, flex her muscles, get political, and talk or walk like a man. She simply extended him an enticing invitation to sample what she was serving. Sometimes I wonder if she cut up the fruit and fed it to Adam in bite-size pieces while he reclined on his back, or if she just took a bite, closed her eyes in ecstasy, and chewed it slowly until he salivated just imagining how good it must taste. Or perhaps after she had savored the flavor of it herself, she soundlessly pressed the remaining half against his lips and gave him an encouraging smile...this would truly be invitation enough. On that note, I submit to you that as a woman, there are ways to influence a man to bite, and there are ways to influence a man to bite. By God's design, he'll be putty in your hands. By your own determination, you'll be met with great resistance. If you do manage to get your way, the consequences of your ill-gotten victory could erase any smidgen of satisfaction you experience short-term. A backlash occurs every time we women step out of the original blue-print, and that backlash creates suffering.

Have you ever noticed that the stronger women become, the more resistance men give, becoming more abusive and more physically demanding. Masculine women cause men to dig in their heels and fight for their positions. They're not only fighting for their positions, they are fighting for their own self-respect, for their right to live up to what their spirit knows is the calling of a man. I believe that men have become more physically abusive and demanding of sexual favors because this is the only time they feel in control. I don't know of a delicate way to say this, so I'll just say it and hope it doesn't get the best of you. Taking control is the only time men feel they are once again on top, if you'll pardon the pun. We women, in turn, then begin to bargain with our bodies. This is a power play that results in painful repercussions in the long run. I believe that if women redis-covered the art and the power of their own femininity, thus releasing men to be the men they were created to be, these negative acts of affirming their identity as men—through abuse and intimidation—would no longer be an option. God's original design put back into play would abort all of these retaliatory tactics that keep our relationships in the state of a no-win contest.

If we keep in mind that man is made in the image of God, then we must realize that his heart also seeks the same thing that God's heart seeks—worship. This eradicates the concept that man's primary desire is for sexual intimacy and replaces it with the truth that man's foremost desire is for honor, honor that comes in the form of respect and sub-mission. This train of thought is consistent throughout Scripture.

"Wives, submit yourselves unto your own husbands, as unto the Lord. For the husband is the head of the wife, even as Christ is the head of the church: and he is the saviour of the body. Therefore as the church is subject unto Christ, so let the wives be to their own husbands in every thing" (Ephesians 5:22-24 KJV).

"...for the Father seeketh such to worship him. God is a Spirit: and they that worship him must worship him in spirit and in truth" (John 4:23,24 KJV).

"But thou art holy, O thou that inhabitest the praises of Israel" (Psalm 22:3 KJV).

God dwells in the midst of His praise, and it is clear that intimacy is born out of the worship experience. Why is this? Because all barriers come down in the face of admiration. All defenses are lowered as we enjoy the attributes of our beloved, and they in turn respond by drawing closer to us. As our praises go up to God, He comes down, drawing closer and standing ready to pour out to us the desires of our heart. The same thing takes place in our mortal relationships. As we make men feel good about themselves, they pour more of themselves out to us. True intimacy is birthed out of this sort of communion, and sexual intimacy is the highest form of mutual worship. It is the place of complete vulnerability and openness. For a moment suspended in time man and woman return to being naked and unashamed. Without pretense all is revealed and exchanged, and the two come away with a deeper knowing of one another, sharing a bond stronger than before. This was God's perfect design for relationships.

As they preach submission from the pulpit, men often overlook one very crucial fact: Love inspires submission and

submission inspires more love. The commands of God create
a chain reaction as He admonishes husbands to love their
wives as Christ loved the church and instructs wives to
submit to their husbands. It is much easier to submit to
someone who is constantly pouring out his love on you. It is
much easier to submit to a person who gives sacrificially, a
person you trust has your best interest at heart. Only a man
submitted to Christ can do this. So submission within a marriage actually begins with the man being submitted to God.
The whole household must be submitted to someone greater
than themselves or you've got trouble. This is why I always
counsel women to decide, *before* they get married, whether or
not they respect the man they are considering as a marriage
partner enough to submit to him. If you marry that man and
then decide he is an idiot to whom you don't want to listen,
God will still hold you accountable for being disobedient.
Don't ignore the signs while you are still free to make an
informed choice. Do yourself a favor—don't get married and
then start flexing your muscles. It will only make both of you
miserable, and it's just too exhausting in the long run.
Remember, partnership should reduce stress, not heighten it.

It's a Woman Thing

With all of life's pressures surrounding us, how do we find
our way back to the garden? How do we get back to the place
of women being women and men being men and nobody
minding? How do we return to celebrating our differences
and making them work for *all* of us? The serpent has woven
an intricate lie into the fabric of our existence. He has made
us believe that if we are not "as" another, then we are "less"
than the other. What a ridiculous concept! A dollar bill has

the same value as a dollar coin, doesn't it? Each will buy the same thing. So men use authority while women use influence. Men are calculating while women are instinctual. Men are fixers while women are nurturers. We could go on and on with the comparisons, but the bottom line is that both elements of what a man has to offer and what a woman has to offer are just as vital as the other to the existence of us all.

So what's so awful about just being a woman? Absolutely nothing! Women are powerful and magnificent. They are intelligent and wonderful. Beautiful and mysterious. Small wonder we drive men to distraction. Woman is one of the most complex creations that God fashioned. Every time a baby enters the world through a woman's womb, and a mother feeds that child from her breast, the earth should stop for a moment of respectful silence. But then we wouldn't get a whole lot done, would we? And so the world continues to turn, miracles are taken for granted, and the value of womanhood is overlooked, mixed in with all the usual business of the day.

How do we separate the woman, the wife, the mother, from the business mogul? How do we remain feminine and still get respect? Obviously, it's possible. The virtuous woman in the Bible did it and everyone at her house seemed happy. What did she know that we don't? I think she knew she was pivotal to effecting change in her world.

Change Begins at Home

The bottom line is this—women are not powerless to make a difference. The secret is hidden within our femininity, the unique giftings of our womanhood, the precious treasure so many of us have lost along the way. So let's start at the beginning, pick up the pieces, and work through this thing together. In the following chapters we will not point our fingers at men and proclaim what they are doing wrong. Instead, we'll take an introspective look at ourselves and find the best ways to get back on the right track. I have always found that changes *around* me began *within* me. It does truly begin with us. I believe it also begins with us being comfortable with who we are as women, being aware of our own uniqueness and value.

It is time to get rid of the inferiority complex. It is time to stop trying to force others to take us seriously. It is time to develop a sense of humor. (Security always gives us that.) Laughter in the face of ignorance has always shifted the power from the bully to the potential victim. What you think of yourself will determine how others respond to you. Confidence has a way of drawing its own invisible boundaries to insulate us from bad manners and perverted standards. It is time to get over ourselves, too. I believe that when we take ourselves too seriously, no one else will ever take us seriously enough in our own eyes. This is the deception of pride. Pride is too expensive. It costs us our peace. And it always costs us valuable relationships and wonderful opportunities (sometimes ones we're unaware of). Life is not supposed to be a contest; it is a journey. We would all enjoy the ride so much more if we weren't worried about getting credit for reaching the destination and simply celebrated the trip instead. It is time for us to stop seeking validation from without and to reclaim it from within.

Being a feminine woman is not synonymous with being a weak woman. Femininity has gotten a bad rap in recent decades. When women started burning their bras (at a time when I was simply wishing I had a reason to wear one!) and screaming about equality, we lost something valuable—we lost sight of treasuring who we were and delighting in all we had to offer. Somewhere along the way we swallowed the "woman is inferior" lie—hook, line, and sinker. As a matter of fact, we feasted on this misconception more than those we accused of instituting it did. And the lie grew as it rolled

Femininity is definitely strength under control. Femininity is strength wrapped in a velvet glove. It doesn't insist on its own way, but most of the time it gets it.

down the mountain of our self-esteem. It was joined by other lies and together they became an avalanche, adding additional variations on the theme of the lie along the way, such as the deception that being feminine means being powerless. Or the wrong idea that we are not valuable and therefore are unqualified to be taken seriously. That is a lie. I don't know a man on the face of this earth who doesn't take his mother, or her words, seriously. Case closed.

The word "feminine" has many synonyms when you check the thesaurus—female, womanly, ladylike, woman-like, non-masculine, unmanly, endowed with womanly qualities, soft, gentle, delicate, sensitive, modest, effeminate. Webster says that someone feminine will "have the quality or nature of the female sex, characteristic of or appropriate or peculiar to women." I would like to interject that I term feminine as synonymous with meek, which in the Greek is defined as "strength under control." Femininity is definitely strength under control. Femininity is strength wrapped in a velvet glove. It doesn't insist on its own way, but most of the time it gets it.

Femininity is not casting coy looks out from behind a fan. It is not wearing little lace gloves, or swooning in the face of the slightest indiscretion. It is an inner quality that emanates from a woman who knows her calling and her value. Feminine women are strong women because their influence is deeply felt. This influence gets beneath the surface because it is invited in. It is invited in because it is attractive and nonthreatening. It is nonthreatening because it doesn't seek to intimidate. You see, the feminine woman knows who she is and celebrates being all woman. She lets who she is naturally do all the work for her. Men fall all over themselves for that woman. And those women are happy, stress-free women.

I love being a woman. I love all that it encompasses. I love the fact that I can be a bundle of contradictions without shame. That I can be intelligent. Intuitive. Sharply discerning. Dignified and strong or soft and warm. Generous with my compassion. Tender with my touch. That I can cry openly. That I can ask a man to carry something when it's heavy and enjoy his gallantries. I revel in the knowledge that it's my prerogative to change my mind a million times 'cause it's a woman thing. It's a beautiful thing. As far back as I can remember, I have wonderful memories of my mother's femininity. She had the miraculous talent of juggling all the affairs of the family—and yet she was so…feminine! She cooked. And I'm talking serious cooking, all types of exotic dishes. You never knew which country your food was coming from on any given day of the week. On Saturdays there would be a line outside the door awaiting her fresh-baked bread and cinnamon rolls. She sewed, too—my clothes, her clothes, and even things for Daddy. She did hair, and believe you me, doing mine was quite a chore. Our house was always so spotless you could eat off the floor. She went to work…whew! Girlfriend, she was busy! And on top of all of that, I cannot recall my mother with a hair out of place. She always smelled good. She always looked beautiful and made Daddy and me look beautiful, too.

Now, man was definitely king at our house. My father had the last word. No discussion. But there was no mistaking who was queen, either. My mother's influence was definitely felt. They were a united front, a mighty force not to be crossed or disobeyed. They had each other's backs. They made their agreements in private and stuck to them. I believe that because my dad's manhood was never questioned, resisted, or threatened, he was free to be openhanded with my mother. He never had to remind her that he was boss, try to throw his weight around, or clamp down on her because then he would have been in a war all by himself. No, he was great to her. They were a team, picking up each other's slack. He would cook if she couldn't, never hesitating to assist with any other chore that needed attention. Today they are closer than ever. His word still stands and she still basks beneath his protection.

I never got the sense that my mother ever felt inferior to or controlled by my father. She filled her role and he filled his because the vacuum was left for him to rise to the occasion. Perhaps she knew instinctively that men abdicate any duty you do not give them room to do. She simply allowed him to be who he was, while being quite comfortable being who she was, right down to the little things.

I have been fussing with my mother for years, telling her that she really needs to learn how to pump her own gas. Yet she seems to draw immense pleasure from the fact that her husband will do it when it needs to be done. Talk about Southern Belle syndrome! This causes the '90s woman in me to fall down on the floor and writhe in agony, screaming, "This is a disgrace! How can you be so helpless? What would happen if he dropped dead tomorrow?" But she doesn't see it that way. Her train of thought is, why should she do it if he's there to do it? And, hey, who am I to interrupt her program? She is perfectly happy with their arrangement. And so is he because he feels needed. And on that note, neither one of them is going anywhere. They've found their rhythm. They're connected for life.

I think that each of us women must find our own individual way. Some of us will pump gas and some of us will not. As for me personally, I want my coat held, my chair pulled out, doors opened, grade-A precious vessel treatment all the way! I'm not ruining my manicure unnecessarily; why should I if I don't have to? Anyway you look at it, the bottom line is really this—are you reveling in being the woman God created you to be? If this issue still seems a bit insulting to you, if I'm ruffling your feathers…good! Read on. Read on with an open spirit. And as we examine the concept of rediscovering our femininity by digging into specific areas in which we are tempted to take up a mantle that is not ours to wear, be honest with yourself about where you've lost your way. Remember, this is ultimately about your own personal liberation. Letting go of every fantasy about who you think you are supposed to be is the first step to freedom.

Perhaps you've dug in the heels of your stiletto pumps and screamed, "Why is it that the woman always has to be the one to get her act together while the man is free to continue being a buffoon? When is God going to give him a wake-up call?" I believe the answer is best put in the words of my friend Rebecca Osaigbovo, who wrote a book called *Chosen Vessels.* She said, "Adam is asleep." As the revelation of that sunk into my spirit, I let out a scream. That was rich! Rebecca continued to unfold this train of thought and make it plain. You see, God made Adam go into a deep sleep in order to create woman. He didn't awaken Adam until woman was a complete and finished work. God is waiting for you to become a finished vessel of honor—one capable of being the catalyst to making that man change his ways because of your blameless behavior.

> "Wives, fit in with your husbands' plans; for then if they refuse to listen when you talk to them about the Lord, they will be won by your respectful, pure behavior. Your godly lives will speak to them better than any words" (1 Peter 3:1,2 TLB).

Before He wakes up that man in your life, God is going to complete His work in you. He is not going to wake the man up to behold a half-baked cookie. He wants every woman to be rooted and grounded in the full understanding of who she was created to be prior to setting her before the eyes of her own Adam. She needs to be equipped to inspire that man to be the man he's supposed to be. God knows that a complete woman is a force with which to be reckoned. This is why He pitted the woman, not the man, against the devil. He said that He would place enmity between the woman and the snake, between her offspring and the snake's offspring (Genesis 3:15). He knew that a determined woman was capable of doing great damage to the kingdom of darkness, especially if she sensed that any of her beloved were being threatened. Women are powerful. And praying women are the most dangerous weapons on the planet in Satan's eyes. When a God-fearing, Jesus-knowing woman prays, everybody needs to grab their seat belts, because there's gonna be a whole lotta shakin' goin' on until her request is fulfilled.

That's what I'm talking about. Getting back to God's original design. Moving and walking, not after the flesh but after the spirit. Then, and only then, will our men sit up, take notice, and get in line. It's up to us, ladies. I'm willing to do my part. So what about you? I say it's time to start a Back-to-the-Garden movement. Then and only then will we taste the fruit of absolute victory.

> "For the man is not of the woman; but the woman of the man. Neither was the man created for the woman; but the woman for the man....Nevertheless neither is the man without the woman, neither the woman without the man, in the Lord. For as the woman is of the man, even so is the man also by the woman; but all things of God" (1 Corinthians 11:8,9,11,12 KJV).

Heavenly Father, help us get back to basics to rediscover the beauty of whom You created us to be. To rediscover our value in the light of the fact that in Your eyes there is neither male

nor female, Greek nor Jew, for You created us all for Your good pleasure. You've bought us with the price of the blood of Your Son Jesus and ransomed us to be Yours. And in this we find our greatest validation—that we are heirs together with Him in heavenly places and walk in dominion in this present life because You shed Your love on us. Grant us the security to remember at all times who we are and Whose we are. Grant us the peace to know that our rights are all hidden in You and You are the ultimate defender of our cause. Finish the work that You've begun in us. Make us worthy vessels. Make us complete in You according to Your design. Help us to rest in the assurance that as we yield to being the women You long for us to be, You will honor our submission by crowning us with Your divine favor and blessing us with abundant fulfillment and joy. In Jesus' name. Amen.

THREE

Taking the Lead

Wisdom spread her skirts
and sat beneath the tree
tucking prudence and insight
beneath her feet
she flung discretion
around her shoulders
to ward off the chill
of foolishness
and waited
for those who were willing to listen to come
the invitation had been voiced
that all who chose
the way of life should come
come and drink
of what she served
she waited
not insisting
not vaunting herself
on unwelcoming ears
for she knew that
time would tell
the fulfillment
of her words
and so she waited
basking in the light she had been given
allowing it to keep her secure
in all she knew
and when she spoke
her words were not wasted
they fell on the
fertile ground of thirsty hearts

that came craving refreshment
diamonds were given to only those
who recognized their value
for wisdom did not waste the gifts of God
on the undiscerning
saving them from stumbling
on self-imposed offenses
for wisdom knew that
timing was everything...

*D*eborah the prophetess sat beneath the palm, looking out over the countryside. The line was beginning to form. The Israelites were gathering to have their disputes settled, but Deborah had a more urgent matter on her heart than all those who were waiting to present their matters to her. "Mother," the first in line began. As Deborah listened, she kept her eye on the horizon, searching for the first sign of Barak. When he appeared, she gently dispersed those gathered, assuring them that she would hear their case another day. For she needed to attend to a matter that must be discussed for the good of them all.

Studying the man who now stood before her, Deborah chose her words wisely. Though she was judge of all of Israel, she remained sensitive to the spirits of the men God instructed her to address. Perhaps it was this gentle respect that caused them to follow her willingly in a society that was not used to women in leadership. She tilted her head a little to the left to cut off the sun's glare that interrupted her view of Barak's face. Then she asked him in an almost quizzical manner, "Hasn't the Lord God of Israel commanded you to muster an army at Mount Tabor and take ten thousand men of Naphtali and of the Zebulun tribe? And hasn't He told you that He in return will lure Sisera, the captain of Jabin's army, with his chariots and multitude and deliver him into your hand?" She allowed the silent question, "What are you waiting for?" to hang between them.

Beneath her steady gaze that held no judgment, Barak felt no hesitancy to answer, "If you will go with me, then I will go. But if you will not go with me, then I will not go." Again she studied him, wondering how he would receive her next statement. "All right, I will go with you," she said. "But you need to know that because you've chosen to go about things this way, you've sacrificed the honor that could have been yours. The glory for this victory will now go to a woman." Barak bowed in acquiescence and Deborah arose to go with him. Well, as history records it, between the natural elements causing poor weather conditions and the determination of the Israelite troops, the armies of Sisera were routed. Sisera himself fled on foot, arriving at the tent of Jael, the wife of Heber, and accepted her invitation to hide in her tent. As he lay resting, she drove a tent peg through his skull and killed him, thus fulfilling Deborah's prophecy that the glory of the victory would go to a woman. However, she magnanimously had Barak join her in singing the victory song, giving the glory to God and noting all the participants of the battle.

I suppose I am intrigued with the story of Deborah because her life flies in the face of a lot of present-day theology dealing with the place of women in the church. Deborah is one of the best-kept secrets in the Bible, perhaps because her life and role in history raise some very real questions. If women are to keep silent in the church, how did this woman end up being a judge over Israel? Kinda makes you go hmm, doesn't it? The Bible very clearly states that God selected the judges.

> "And when the LORD raised them up judges, then the LORD was with the judge, and delivered them out of the hand of their enemies all the days of the judge..." (Judges 2:18 KJV).

The Bible also clearly states that the people followed Deborah willingly. In fact, Barak refused to go into battle without her! So much for women keeping silent in the church. But before you get too excited about this liberating revelation, I think it is important to take a closer look at Deborah and discover how she operated. Her life holds important keys for those of us who wonder how to remain feminine yet maintain any type of significant power in the boardroom, in the home, or even in the ministry.

Deborah is listed in Judges 4:4 as first a prophetess—her spiritual calling before birth, then as the wife of Lappidoth—her natural calling as a woman, and finally as judge of Israel—her positional call as a servant of God. Though Deborah was the reigning authority in the land, she was a woman under authority—under authority to the Lord and to her husband. She was called a "mother" to Israel. This paints a very vivid picture of a woman whom many saw as not only a wise sage who truly heard the word of the Lord, but a woman who had a heart with enough room to nurture a wounded nation back to health. She was a comfort to the people—honest, uncompromising, and forthright, yet gentle and nonthreatening. You kind of get the idea that people could take the truth from her without becoming offended. Perhaps this was because she waited until they asked, unless she was prompted by God. But I think it had more to do with the fact that she did not insist on having her own way. She understood the word "service." She understood God's view of authority.

God had elevated Deborah to the place of judge because she was first called the wife of Lappidoth. The greatest leaders are those who have allowed themselves to be led. She could be trusted with this position because she placed first things first. This is evident in her discussion with Barak. She didn't preach, walk, or talk like a man. She was a woman living out her calling. She was sensitive to the male ego, as well as to God's purposes. She handed the battle to him; he asked for her assistance. She in turn agreed to go as he had asked, but gave him the option to change his mind by letting him know the end his request implied. Was he willing to have it go down in history that a woman had won the war? He was, and so they proceeded. Still, when they reached the battlefield, she instructed him when to go forth and fight. She didn't go charging ahead of everyone; she gave Barak the prompting and left the fighting to the men. Though a woman was finally responsible for the demise of the enemy's captain, Deborah didn't gloat, "I told you so." Rather, she gave Barak gracious credit for the part he played, and then she moved on. This was a woman who was seasoned from years of being a godly wife. As God observed her behavior toward her husband, He knew that He could trust her as judge over Israel.

The Road to Freedom

I doubt very seriously that if Deborah had had a reputation as a rebellious wife who ran her husband, the people would have respected her the way in which they did. They would have resented her and resisted her leadership. No one likes to see a henpecked man, not even in the liberal society in which we live. Just think of those in leadership and the snickers that accompany the comments that their wives are really running the show. God knew He could not put a woman like that in power. The leader He chose had to be one who would walk as an example of His divine order. It's a simple lesson, but a deep one. The more we yield, the more we are released to be elevated.

I was tested on this very principle as I began this chapter, and laughed to myself through gritted teeth that I hadn't "arrived" as much as I would have liked. Though I understand the principle, it's a whole different matter to put it into practice. Perhaps from my years of being single and independent, the notion of reporting in eludes my understanding from time to time. In any event, there's never a good excuse for not being accountable. Not being accountable always ends in disaster, I can assure you. But in this particular situation, I was working on a project for a client. We had disagreed on some of the details, so on that note I decided to just forge ahead and put everything in place to my own liking and worry about selling him on it later. After all, *I* was the one with the great imagination and I couldn't help it if he just didn't get it. Of course, he would like it when I was finished!

Well, the whole thing blew up in my face as my client's client didn't get it, either. When the results got back to my client, he exploded. As I set about the business of trying to put this whole mess back into some kind of salvageable form, I was convicted of stepping out from under his authority. As I humbled myself and asked his forgiveness for moving ahead of him without keeping him informed of what I was doing, he became my partner in fighting for what I wanted. Once he knew he could trust me to keep him in the loop of what was happening, he released me to continue the project in the way I saw fit. I kind of snickered heavenward and said, "All right, Lord, You're right. I do get too big for my britches from time to time." It wasn't about my ability to do fabulous work without my client's input. That was never in question. It was about having a respect for the order of how things should be done.

There is no way around God's order of authority. It is for our own protection. Within the confines of submission we are released for profound influence and leadership. Every time we rebel, we become a servant to what we try to rise against. This is what happened in the garden. This is where the role of husband and wife becomes sadly misinterpreted by the insecure who choose to wave their Bibles around in defense of their abuse of power. This is also where women become offended and more tempted than ever to override this misinterpretation by taking their lives into their own hands while accusing God of being this Omnipotent Macho Spirit giving men license to make life difficult for women. I get this picture of God in my mind, brows raised, shoulders hunched, palms held upward, saying, "Hey, you got it all wrong! I'm trying to keep you covered, but you're making My job really difficult."

Oh, Curses!

It is time to take an honest look at what being out of order costs us as women. It costs us the covering and protection of confident men. It costs us the security of our homes and the soundness of our children. It costs us the safety of our communities. It costs us our personal peace and fulfillment. It costs us our health. Yes, even our health. As female health problems escalate, I have pondered this dilemma, wondering what was the contributing factor. And I received a stunning revelation from the Lord. Let's look at the original curse following the fall.

> "Unto the woman he said, I will greatly multiply thy sorrow and thy conception; in sorrow thou shalt bring forth children; and thy desire shall be to thy husband, and he shall rule over thee. And unto Adam he said, Because thou hast hearkened unto the voice of thy wife, and hast eaten of the tree, of which I commanded thee, saying, Thou shalt not eat of it: cursed is the ground for thy sake; in sorrow shalt thou eat of it all the days of thy life; thorns also and thistles shall it bring forth to thee; and thou shalt eat the herb of the field; in the sweat of thy face shalt thou eat bread, till thou return unto the ground; for out of it wast thou taken..." (Genesis 3:16-19 KJV).

In other words, what was supposed to be easy will now be difficult. The thing that gives you the most joy will also give you the most pain. I always like to dig a little deeper, so as I look at these passages, I see more than the usual summation that women would experience pain during the delivery process. I see this as a perpetual state of difficulty beyond the initial birth of a child. The Bible makes several references throughout to women weeping over, or being in a state of sorrow over, their children. "Bringing forth" children has proven to be more and more difficult as time goes by. We are waging war with the media, the educational system, other wayward children, and outside influences to keep the minds and spirits of our own children pure. This reduces many a mother to tears as she ponders the solution to the preservation of her children. Yet none of this causes her to draw back from her husband. She is still drawn to the comfort of intimacy with him, even knowing what that intimacy has the capacity to produce.

Let's revisit the text of Genesis 3:16, which states, "Your desire will be for your husband, and he will rule over you" (NIV). The Hebrew offers us a clearer understanding of the "R" word so misused in many a denomination, and will help you get it once and for all. Literally, this translation states that because of the turning of your heart to your husband (and, by implication, away from God) for validation, completion, and affirmation, he shall rule over you. This is the case with anything or anyone that we rely on other than God for our sense of self. That thing or person then begins to rule our lives. The love of money, power, food, materialism—you name it, it will rule over you if you let it outrun God in the area of your affections. This was Eve's dilemma. I will reiterate that this is not just a married woman's issue. It affects single women, too. Remember, this was a universal curse. It included all women. Look at how women today are ruled by the desire to get a man, have a man, and keep a man. How many waking moments are spent laboring over this issue with friends or alone? How many women have settled for unhappy relationships merely because they've come to the sad conclusion that to have *some* man is better than *no* man at all? The words of the prophet are being played out in modern-day scenarios the world over.

> "In that day seven women will take hold of one man and say, 'We will eat our own food and provide our own clothes; only let us be called by your name. Take away our disgrace!'" (Isaiah 4:1 NIV).

Another translation says, "Take away our reproach." It is interesting to note that it was not until after the fall that Adam named Eve. Before she was created Adam had named all living things in the garden, yet Eve seemingly remained unnamed. Why? Because God had named her. A name is the definition of who you are. God is very fussy about names. We see throughout Scripture His participation in naming babies according to His purpose for their lives. Now, after the fall, it was man who gave woman her definition, according to her heart's desire, by naming her. Today women still crave to be "named" by a man. Now hear this: You don't have to wait for a man to define who you are. God has already given you a name!

> "No longer will they call you Deserted, or name your land Desolate. But you will be called Hephzibah (my delight is in her), and your land Beulah (married)....
> as a bridegroom rejoices over his bride, so will your God rejoice over you" (Isaiah 62:4,5 NIV).

Because of God, a woman is a complete woman whether she has a man or not. The Lord is a husband to the husbandless. And that's some husband to have! He's One who owns everything you could ever dream of or hope for. We're talking about having the wealthiest husband in the world! "For your Maker is your Husband—the LORD Almighty is his name—the Holy One of Israel is your Redeemer" (Isaiah 54:5 NIV).

Let's move on. While man's greatest joy comes from achievement, he would now have to labor by the sweat of his brow to gain that sense of fulfillment. So in the end man and woman sinned by eating, and now they would have to suffer in order to eat. Eve influenced Adam to sin, and now they would be forever locked in a battle of wills. Their attempt to become all-knowing, "like God" apart from God, gained them the sentence of their bodies no longer being eternal "like God" but returning back to the dust from whence they came. Though this might seem like a cruel reminder to clarify who was whom in the mix of man versus God, this was really God's gracious way of giving us an escape from a perpetually difficult life.

What, then, is the stunning disclosure? If Jesus took all the curses on the tree, then what's all the fuss about? Well, unfortunately, just because He wrote the check, it doesn't mean that everyone has cashed it. And we all know that a check is just a check until it is redeemed by the recipient. It seems that most women have not only not "cashed" the check of freedom from the curse they were given concerning childbirth and man, they've also gone one step further. They have added the curse of Adam on top of the original curse they already embrace. More than ever, we have women killing themselves in the workplace, toiling by the sweat of their brows. This was not God's original design. Our bodies were never made to be exposed to such an intense measure of stress. The "superwoman syndrome" is taking its toll on us in larger and larger waves, thus the rise in female health problems. Notice where many of these problems strike—in the reproductive organs that produce our children, as well as the breasts that nurture our children, piggybacking on top of the curse concerning childbearing. The enemy is subtle. Or is he really so subtle? After all, we've opened the door and invited him to strike us at the core of who we are as women.

Now, don't get defensive. I, too, am among the guilty, not by choice, but by what I get sucked into believing is necessity. The common belief—and in great part it's a reality—is

that in light of the times and most of our personal circumstances, "a woman's got to do what a woman's got to do" to
survive. This is all part and parcel of what the sin factor
delivers to our door. We must be careful, however, not to
blame God for what is a natural consequence of man's bad
choices. I use the word "man" in the collective sense. The
bad choice that we make is submitting to the enemy's trick
of utilizing masculine tactics in the marketplace.

By the time we are finished being "men" at the office, we
find it difficult to shift back to being women at home. You
see, I don't believe that God is against women working and
being successful, à la "the virtuous woman." It is when we
get out of order that we get in trouble. We must watch the

When we lose ourselves as women and begin forcing ourselves to develop muscles we're not designed to have, our internal and relational system suffers.

---

motivations of our heart and our posture as women when we
venture out into the world.

When we lose ourselves as women and begin forcing ourselves to develop muscles we're not designed to have, our internal and relational system suffers. This is where Deborah rose above the curse. In today's society she probably would have been labeled a feminist, but in reality she was far from it.

Femininity vs. Feminism

I think the subtlety of Satan would be laughable if it wasn't so dangerous. I'll give you an example. The "feminist movement" is not about empowering women to be feminine; it uses masculine tactics to achieve its agenda. Get it? Feminism—which is anything but feminine—does not stand for femininity, which is where a woman's true power lies. Though it pursues some causes that most of us would consider honorable, it masks an agenda that is far more sinister than the masses, or even some of the movement's leaders, could believe.

In the end, "feminism" will do us all more harm than good. Anytime a power struggle takes place between two opposing forces, any so-called "movement" that operates under any form of sexism becomes divisive at best. This is a mode of transportation we cannot afford if we really desire to reach a relational destination. Once we're all on the bandwagon of "feminism," we will find ourselves heading in the opposite direction of where we really wanted to go.

Some say the "feminist movement" is a lesbian movement masked with a few honorable agendas to seduce the masses. After all, who would argue with equal pay for equal work? But women going off to fight in wars and leaving babies at home? It seems that the main women fighting for abortion rights are not interested in ever having children, anyway. I find this very disturbing. How far do we push the envelope in the name of equal rights? And do you really want to do

everything that men do? These are important questions you
need to ask yourself. Or perhaps you just see feminism as
being able to do certain things if you wanted to do them.
But that begs the question, don't you have better things to do
with your time than battle over issues that have no urgent
relevance to your world?

In short, I must say that I feel the "feminist movement" is
out of control. Its charisma and passion for defending the
rights of women have distracted us from noticing the frac-
tions it is causing in the basic, everyday exchanges between
men and women. All movements are dangerous when they
result in fighting in the flesh. As spiritual women, we must
forever be cognizant of the fact that we battle "not against
flesh and blood, but against principalities" (Ephesians 6:12
KJV). Lasting victory over any issue in our life will only be
gained as we war in the spirit. God is the true champion of
liberation; we must submit our causes to Him.

For those of you who are confused at the anger you witness
from the "feminist" camp, it is important to note that anger
usually masks extreme pain. It is not conducive to the healing
process to simply conclude that these angry women are all les-
bians and treat them as castaways with no hope of redemp-
tion. No one is beyond the hope of healing and deliverance.
But you must know the seed that the enemy has planted in
order to know how to uproot it. The first fact that many miss
is that lesbianism is born out of a relational void. It is innate
within the longing for love gone out of control. I believe that
a lot of women have resorted to seeking out each other for
comfort, companionship, and physical stimulation simply
because they have grown weary of trying to make it work
with men.

It is important to be educated in this area because we have women sitting in churches all across this land who are hurting, dying quietly inside because they cannot approach anyone in the church for counsel. They fear the disdain and disapproval of other Christians as they struggle with their urges toward other women. In order to minister effectively to those you know who are involved in this lifestyle, you must understand that lesbianism is not a sexual issue; it is an emotional and spiritual one. Women connect to one another in a very powerful way because of their nurturing skills. Men do not connect on this level; therefore, the motivation for homosexual behavior comes from a different place—it is based on visual stimulation and sensuality. But that, of course, would be another book. Whereas a man is able to separate his sexuality from his emotions, a woman's emotions and sexuality are closely tied together. When the men in a woman's world abuse her physically or are incapable of fulfilling her emotionally, the danger exists for the spirit of deception to enter into her life. Thereby she will mistake the emotional fulfillment she receives from other women in her life as a source of eros (sexual) love. This danger grows into a reality if the woman is not cognizant of the fact that no man or woman can ever completely fulfill her emotionally. Only God can do that.

Women who seek immediate gratification for their longings will fall prey to this deception, and the spirit of lesbianism will grip them. These are women who simply don't want to try anymore. It has become easier for them to say that men are not their preference in order to maintain a level of self-satisfaction. They are filled with pain and unbelief and have resorted to ungodly means in order to comfort themselves. They would never admit this, but they have thumbed their noses at God, refusing the comfort and emotional fulfillment that only He can offer on the level they seek it. And they have turned to other external sources to fill the void in their hearts and emotions. They have chosen to take their destinies into their own hands, to do whatever is necessary to take hold of what they crave—love and fulfillment. On a certain level, this is understandable. I have jokingly said to my best friend, "Too bad you're not a man; I would marry you." But trust me, there is nothing funny about it to God. He designed man and woman to walk together in a way no two men or two women can. To step outside of this order causes dangerous cracks in the foundation of God's blueprint for the kingdom.

Now before you get all excited and accuse me of being judgmental, let me assure you that this is not the Gospel According to Michelle. This is the Gospel According to God, if you will allow me to cite a few key scriptures here in order to solidify my point.

> "Yes, they knew God, but they wouldn't worship him as God or even give him thanks. And they began to think up foolish ideas of what God was like. The result was that their minds became dark and confused....So God let them go ahead and do whatever shameful things their hearts desired. As a result, they did vile and degrading things with each other's bodies. Instead of believing what they knew was the truth about God, they deliberately chose to believe lies....That is why God abandoned them to their shameful desires. Even the women turned against the natural way to have sex and instead indulged in sex with each other....When they refused to acknowledge God, he abandoned them to their evil minds

and let them do things that should never be done....
They are fully aware of God's death penalty for those
who do these things, yet they go right ahead and do
them anyway. And, worse yet, they encourage others
to do them, too" (Romans 1:21-32 NLT).

Now in all fairness, there are people in my life whom I
love dearly and unconditionally who are living what is now
called an "alternative" lifestyle. I am able to sympathize with
the feelings they voice about their situation while making
my stand on the subject crystal-clear. Some of these dear
friends have a background of childhood physical abuse.
Others feel that they were just born that way, while some
simply do not feel comfortable with the opposite sex. This is
an area where Satan has done some of his most successful
work in the area of deception.

Those not in this camp could get sucked into finding their
outlook reasonable if the Word of God wasn't present to say
otherwise. As understandable as all of these explanations
may be, if you choose to agree with those who defend themselves by saying they are "just doing the best they can with
the lot they've been given in life," the bottom line truth is
that God still calls this sin. And He graciously offers a way
out if one chooses to take it.

God's perspective, however, does not need to be delivered in veiled disdain or judgmental fervor, but rather with
love and an understanding that the outward mode of behavior covers a deeper need and a level of pain that surpasses
normal discernment. Speaking the truth in love and compassion is important. No one questions the love of a parent
when he or she corrects a child. Everyone understands that
the parent doesn't want the child to indulge in anything that

would be harmful to her. To cite a wrong does not imply that the *person* is unacceptable, just that their *mode of behavior* is not conducive to victorious living. Sin is sin to God, period. From homosexuality to adultery, fornication to lying, stealing to you name it, He hates it all. Why? Because He doesn't want us to hurt ourselves or one another, and He knows the bottom line—though it may be pleasurable for a season, sin ultimately produces death physically, emotionally, and spiritually.

But herein lies the problem because sin is rooted in self-centeredness and rebellion. Sin says, "I want it *my* way and I want it *now!*" When people violate the Word of God, they can choose several ways to work it out. One, they can repent. Or, they can cast blame, go into denial, or find a way to justify their behavior. Notice the closing statement of a passage from Romans: "They encourage others to do them too." If everybody's doing it, then it must be alright, no? Sounds like the beginning of a movement to me! The more people you get to go along with you, the less resistance you'll encounter. Everyone knows that the majority rules. The greater the mass of followers grows collectively, the more the movement is empowered to solidify its position, economically and otherwise. Pretty soon you have an immovable institution in place that uproots and overthrows the foundation of godly principles. And while people who never took the time to understand those who were hurting, or to offer them effective healing, stand wondering how things got so out of control, these same wounded soldiers, numb to their own pain, limp away, dusting off their hands and proclaiming they've won the war.

From Whence You Came

But Deborah won the war without any help from the feminists, and she kept her femininity and her family intact in the midst of it all. How did she do it? How do we do it? How do we come out as winners in what looks like a man's world without getting caught up in the war? I think we can learn several lessons from Deborah.

The first lesson was that Deborah understood her spiritual calling. She was a prophetess. This was not a self-made title; it was her God-ordained purpose. It was the totality of who she was. Therefore, when she spoke, she spoke with authority. When she spoke, people listened because what she said came to pass. This had nothing to do with her being male or female. It had to do with a need God had to expose His heart and His plans to His people. This was a need God knew Deborah had the disposition to fulfill. So many of us spend our time praying for God to open certain doors for our lives, talents, and various efforts. But I wonder, while we have faith in God for the answer to these desires, does God have faith in us to handle what we've asked for properly? Deborah was yielded to the call because Deborah was yielded to God.

> "But know this first of all, that no prophecy of Scripture is a matter of one's own interpretation, for no prophecy was ever made by an act of human will, but men moved by the Holy Spirit spoke from God" (2 Peter 1:20,21 NASB).

Secondly, Deborah understood her call in the natural as a woman, as a wife. The Bible clearly adds the title of "wife of Lappidoth" to her list of credits, which means it was significant to God. Lappidoth means "to shine forth," which speaks of the fact that her husband had a renown reputation of his own. Yet he was secure enough to release Deborah to be the great leader she was. The way she handled the situation with Barak speaks volumes about what went on in her home and the way she interacted with her husband. And it also shows us why Lappidoth remained secure enough to release his wife into the role God had called her to fulfill. So many women in ministry voice the complaint that their husbands have squelched their anointing or have resisted their desire to follow what they believe to be God's call on their lives. But this was not the case with Lappidoth. Why not?

The text serves as a clear indication that Deborah was submitted as a wife to her husband. And she was blessed because of it. Her reputation preceded her in the country. Everyone knew that because her house was in order, they could respect her and follow her. Deborah certainly would have been met with resistance if she had been known as a disrespectful wife. Remember what happened in the book of Esther when Queen Vashti refused to come at the king's command? All of the other men began to worry that if the rumor mill got hold of the news that the first lady didn't listen to her husband, all the other women in the land would also begin to disrespect their husbands. No way were they going to tolerate that! So they rallied against the queen and persuaded the king to dismiss her as an example to the rest of the kingdom. Get the picture?

The people never would have willingly followed Deborah if she were out of line. That would have set a dangerous precedent for families across the land. But Deborah understood the ways and emotions of men. She knew that it was important to a man to lead the way to victory in battle.

Because she understood her spiritual call, she was content to simply deliver the message that Barak should go forth and conquer. When Barak refused to go without her, Deborah still felt it necessary to give him the disclaimer that if she went with him, a female would get credit for the victory. Because of her consideration, Barak was able to yield to her and willingly forfeit what his ego would naturally crave. There was a bigger issue at stake; it wasn't about who received the credit at this stage. It was about their people being freed from their oppressors. Freedom became more important than a claim to fame.

And that is the subtle point which most of us miss. A friend of mine was doing a project with a man who felt she needed his help in order to do it well. She was complaining to me about how much this irritated her. My advice to her was, "Let him help you. It costs you nothing, and you stand to gain everything in the end. So he helps you? You do a good job, he feels he made you. You know that is not true, but where is the harm in him feeling that way? The flip side of the equation is important, too. Because he feels he made you, he now has equity in you. And that means he will be more inclined to keep using you instead of finding someone else to fill your slot. You get more work out of having a little humility, while he walks away feeling good about helping someone. It's a small pittance in exchange for getting what you truly want out of the deal. What would taking credit for doing it on your own get you?" If you make a man your ally, he will never be your foe. But in a world that grasps for constant validation, it is easy to become victims of the original sin—pride.

This is where Satan lost it. He lost the point of his existence. He got hung up on seeing his name in the film's credits instead of rejoicing that it was already clearly evident to everyone around him that he had a leading role. It was just not clear enough to him. God had said that he was the most

---

s women, we lose what we ulti-mately want while skirmishing over the reward of recognition.

---

beautiful of all His creations. He held the coveted position of choir director, but it wasn't enough to be approved of by God. He wanted everyone else's overt praise, worship, and validation. He sought all eyes to be on him, confirming that he was fabulous. You know, all the stuff that we want. But we stand to reap the same end that Lucifer (as he was called at the time) did. When we reach to claim the leading credit, we inevitably lose it all. And as women, we lose what we ultimately want while skirmishing over the reward of recognition. "Your Father who sees in secret will reward you openly" (Matthew 6:6 NKJV).

The Order of Life

But back to Deborah. Deborah was perfectly willing to let a man be a man. Deborah was a wife first before she was a judge. She was a woman first before she was a leader. She was under submission first to God, and then to her husband. Some Christian women get this confused and then wonder why their husbands want nothing to do with God or the church. I will tell you why, plain and simple. No man will ever embrace something with which he feels he is in competition. If you are making the man in your life feel that he has to compete with Jesus or your pastor, you need to repent about this right away. The presence of God in your life should make you a better wife to that man. Stop treating the pastor better than you treat your husband. Whether your husband is saved or unsaved, God still holds you accountable to serve, love, and submit to that man. Please remember that this statement excludes abusive situations. For the most part, when a man feels that God is his ally, he will be open to the concept of drawing closer to Him. It is your job to be the bridge between the two.

The second facet of this is that no man is going to frequent a place in which he feels all the women are in charge. Men are fixers by nature. If there is nothing for them to fix, they move on in search of unconquered territory. This is a radical statement, but a true one. Some of the women in the church need to sit down and force these men to rise to the occasion instead of complaining about their lack of involvement. I recently visited a church where a woman served as the pastor. Her husband was greatly gifted as well, but she was clearly touted as the leader of the ministry. I knew what to expect when I entered the sanctuary, and I was correct. The church was full and there were exactly four men in the whole auditorium. The visiting minister got up and asked, "Where are all the men?" It hurt my heart as I scanned the faces of all the women sitting alone. I knew that many of them were believing God for a mate and wondering where they were going to meet him because he certainly was not sitting in the congregation. The males present were already married. Get the picture? It is time for us to put things back in order. Let's face it—God will use a rock if He has to in order to fulfill His purposes, but it is not His preference. And we as women suffer the most when we perpetuate this mode of behavior.

As for those of you who feel stifled and hindered from ministry because of your mate, take heed. God is never going to put your ministry before your care for your husband. That is unscriptural. It would be going against His own Word, and He is not going to do that. If you will put serving your husband first, you will be amazed at how God will honor your commitment to being obedient. Don't forget that serving your husband is also being obedient to God. Your man is won to God by your behavior. He learns how to submit to God based on the example you set through your submission to him. Let me repeat that. You are the only example your mate receives of how to submit to God. And that's powerful.

I have a friend who has a thriving ministry. She told me she had no intention of being out saving the world while her own household went to hell in a handbasket. Shortly thereafter, she announced that she was cutting back on accepting speaking engagements because she wanted to devote herself to serving her husband more. Well, even I raised my eyebrows when she first told me of her intentions, but God has honored her decision in an astounding way. Though she has accepted fewer bookings, the bookings she now gets are for huge meetings and major events. It's almost as if God said, "All right, since you'll be ministering less often, I'll just compact more people into the few meetings that you do schedule!" So in essence, she is actually ministering to more people than if she had run around the country every weekend speaking at smaller meetings. As her husband's ministry grows by leaps and bounds, she accompanies him. They even minister together as a team quite often. And of course her husband is loving every minute of it, hanging all over her with so much love in his eyes that those looking on have to repent of being jealous. Girlfriend has got the best of both worlds because she voted to do things God's way instead of getting hung up on herself.

This is why I have a problem with the new philosophy, "I'm not selfish, I'm self-full." Whatever that means! What's the difference between being selfish and full of self? They are one in the same. They are both opposed to what God teaches. Don't believe the hype; you've simply been served up a new word to make you feel better about being selfish. You know itching ears will get you in trouble. I understand the intent is to heighten your self-esteem, but that's the wrong way to arrive at your destination. You've got to go the God route. In case you need a little extra help being convinced that self-full is not endorsed by the Holy Ghost Administration, consider what God Himself has to say on the subject:

> "Whosoever will come after me, let him deny himself, and take up his cross, and follow me. For whosoever will save his life shall lose it; but whosoever shall lose his life for my sake and the gospel's, the same shall save it" (Mark 8:34,35 KJV).

> "Therefore, I urge you, brothers [sisters], in view of God's mercy, to offer your bodies as living sacrifices, holy and pleasing to God—this is your spiritual act of worship [which is your reasonable service]" (Romans 12:1 NIV).

"I have been crucified with Christ and I no longer
live, but Christ lives in me. The life I live in the
body, I live by faith in the Son of God, who loved me
and gave himself for me" (Galatians 2:20 NIV).

"God resists the proud, but gives grace to the
humble" (1 Peter 5:5 NKJV).

Need I say more? Many of us have been deceived into
believing that there is no honor in having your house in order.
But in the midst of that order God is released to pave the way
for elevation and promotion in our lives. He can trust us to
remain submitted to His voice no matter how lofty our calling
becomes. The way we submit to visible leadership is a good
indicator of how we will heed invisible authority.

And that brings me to my third point. Deborah understood her positional calling as a servant of God. This is the
master hint on how to maintain your femininity in the
boardroom or whatever environment makes you feel as if you
need to wage a war for equal rights or just humane consideration. Deborah did her job because God said so. It wasn't
about the men around her. It was about a kingdom call, not
her own personal agenda. And because the motivation of her
heart was apparent in her actions, God had her back and
everyone had to line up before her.

"Serve wholeheartedly, as if you were serving the
Lord, not men, because you know that the Lord will
reward everyone for whatever good he [or she] does,
whether he is slave or free" (Ephesians 6:7,8 NIV).

"When a man's [or a woman's] ways are pleasing to
the LORD, he makes even his [or her] enemies live at
peace with him [or her]" (Proverbs 16:7 NIV).

"Humble yourselves in the sight of the Lord, and He will lift you up" (James 4:10 NKJV).

"No one from the east or the west or from the desert can exalt a man [or a woman]. But it is God who judges: He brings one down, he exalts another" (Psalm 75:6,7 NIV).

Is that enough proof that your fate does not lie in the hands or opinion of another man? Stop looking at the natural man at your job. Your identity is hidden somewhere higher than the plaque on your door or your company job description. God has ordained you to operate on three levels—in the spirit, as a woman, and as His servant. As you concentrate on fulfilling His call on your life, you will find yourself walking "in paths of righteousness for his name's sake" (Psalm 23:3 NIV) like David did. As you do that, your job performance will automatically escalate to a place of excellence, and then "men...may see your good works and glorify your Father in heaven" (Matthew 5:16 NKJV). That should be your goal, not what you can get out of doing what you do. As glorifying God and revealing His character through the way you carry yourself in your world become your first priority, all the things your heart craves will rain down upon you. Or you can spend all your energy trying to grasp your desires in your human efforts and live a life of frustration—overworked and underappreciated. But as you get over yourself and over the praise of men, God will reward you richly for developing a servant's heart. This holds true for both a man and a woman. But this is not about them today; this is about you.

"There is neither Jew nor Greek, slave nor free, male
nor female, for you are all one in Christ Jesus. If you
belong to Christ, then you are Abraham's seed, and
heirs according to the promise" (Galatians 3:28,29
NIV).

*Dear Heavenly Father, forgive me for my misplaced priorities.
Forgive me for not celebrating the woman You created me to
be. Forgive me for buying into the lie of the world that I am
inferior, a voice to be ignored, an empty vessel without honor.
Help me to embrace the truth that I am fearfully and wonderfully made, that I am a marvelous work, that my femininity is
a treasure hidden in this earthly vessel. Help me to rejoice in
the gifts You have given me, gifts of influence and wisdom. Stir
up the gifts You've placed within me and make we a wise
steward of all that You have deposited in my spirit. As I strip
off all preconceived notions and worldly labels, redress me
with Your salvation, Your authority, Your validation of all that
I am in You. Teach me to be the woman whom You fashioned
me to be. Guide me in the way that You would have me take
to the praise and honor of Your glory. In Jesus' name. Amen.*

FOUR

'Bout Birthin' Babies

She suckled the child
against her breast
reveling in the warmth of this
her reward from heaven
a tiny innocent
so trusting
even now clinging to her
for its sustenance
it was not just milk
that she gave during
this maternal ritual
it was an impartation
of her spirit
of her heart
of her very soul
the key to their destinies
being released in the breaths
between her prayers
and the fluttering of this infant's heartbeat...
yes, more than a child had been born
purpose had been born
born to a specific end
that would be revealed with time
so even as the babe clung to her
she clung to it
needing its nearness
as much as it needed her
both reveling in the closeness of the other
the quiet exchange of love
that needed no sound to express
its devotion

they drank in
the warmth of one another
lulling them both
into a place of rest
and quiet expectation for miraculous tomorrows...
and within their inner beings
they inexplicably knew
they would always
be there for one another
the mother
and her child
the child
and its mother
inseparable
for they had breathed the same air
shared the same heartbeat
fed from the same source of nourishment
from the beginning
their lives were unexplainably intertwined
this was a bond that could
not be severed...
even if one attempted to deny its existence
the bond would remain
an invisible cord
growing tighter
in times of crisis
of sadness
of transition
of loneliness...
of fear and questions...
growing tighter, yes

but never being severed
for their lives were forever
bound
inside of one another
this mother and child...

A Tale of Three Mothers

*T*his was not a convenient time to have a child. Jochebed drew a deep breath, pressed the child against her breast, and hurried along the back roads that led to the river. "Please Lord, don't let him cry," she silently prayed. It was a miracle she had not been discovered thus far. Her heart pounded louder in her ears every time he had cried during the last three months, and still they had not been detected. In the face of the law that decreed for all male children to be drowned in the Nile, Jochebed vowed that this would not be the fate of her son. If she must break the law, then break the law she would. From the moment she saw his beautiful little face, she knew he was no ordinary child. There was something special about him. She, like every other mother in Israel, prayed that she would give birth to the Redeemer, and she couldn't honestly say as she gazed at this little one that he was the Messiah. All she knew was that his life was worth saving. He was her child. A perfect, beautiful, healthy child, carefully formed by God. How could she allow any harm to come to this gift He had placed in her care? No, she would not allow him to die before he had a chance to embrace his purpose, whatever that might be.

By pure mother's instinct, Jochebed knew that her son's life had to be preserved at all cost. There was something important that this child was born to do. She believed this so fervently that she was willing to give him up in order to secure his future. And so she crept toward the Nile, literally holding her breath all the way. She did not dare exhale until she had safely deposited this most precious parcel in a sealed basket and watched it drift away, carrying its unusual cargo down the river. "Go with God," she breathed, releasing this child who held her heart into the hands of the only One who could keep him safe. As she turned to take the loneliest walk she had ever taken, returning home with empty arms, she resigned herself to the fact that she had done her part. The rest was up to Yahweh.

Truly God had honored her bravery, she concluded, when her daughter came back to report that the Pharaoh's daughter had found the baby Moses floating down the river and adopted him as her own. How ironic that the daughter of the one who had ordered her baby's death would be the one to save his life! And she, Jochebed, had been hired to nurse the child. Her child! What she had willingly sacrificed for the sake of God's higher good had been given back to her with added provision. "Only God," she thought to herself, "only God could twist fate and make it laughable."

In another time and place, Rebekah stood waiting for her son Jacob to return with the ingredients she had told him to gather for the stew. She was determined to assist Jacob in getting the blessing his father had reserved for Esau. It was not that she didn't love Esau, but Jacob had always been her favorite. From the moment he clamored to get out of womb first, determinedly gripping the heel of Esau when he couldn't make his way through ahead of him, Jacob vied for his mother's affections once he arrived in the world. It seemed as if Esau had given up early in life, going in search of consolation in the arms of foreign women as far removed as possible from what his mother was like. This did nothing to endear Rebekah to this son so different from the other. Esau was independent and kept to himself, preferring hunting in the wide-open spaces to spending time underfoot in the household. He gruffly gained his father's approval, while Jacob catered to his mother's affections without any shame. She, in turn, spoiled him rotten, not realizing until far too late that her indulgence would bear them agonizing problems in the future.

But today Rebekah's mind did not dwell on what her well-devised deception would cost her, only on the immediate result. All she knew was that she felt no affection in her heart for those knuckle-headed foreign women Esau had married. And it would be over her dead body that any of them reveled in the benefits that would be theirs if Isaac gave Esau the blessing. The coveted blessing...humph! Esau hadn't even had the sense to treasure his birthright; surely he would have no appreciation of the blessing, either.

Now that Isaac's favorite meal was bubbling over the fire, Rebekah set about the task of wrapping Jacob's arms in goatskin. With a final sigh of resolve, she pushed him toward his father's tent laden down with a fragrant-smelling meal. When Jacob emerged some time later, he looked rather relieved. The ruse had worked. While basking in the wonder of the blessing Jacob had been given, Rebekah's heart rejoiced—she had accomplished her mission. Her elation, however, was short-lived. Esau proved to be much more upset over losing the blessing than they had imagined for one so nonchalant about his birthright. When his dark threats of revenge reached her ears, Rebekah knew the only thing she could do to save Jacob's life would ultimately break her heart. She would be forced to part with her son in order to keep him out of harm's way. Convincing Isaac that Jacob should be sent to her people to find a bride from among them, Rebekah prepared herself for the heartbreak she would experience when her son went on his way.

As Rebekah watched Jacob disappear over the horizon, she died a little more inside with every step he took. She memorized his silhouette, knowing intuitively that this was the last time she would see her most-cherished prize. Perhaps if she had waited and not been so swift to take matters into her own hands, God would have found a way to secure the blessing for Jacob. But now it was too late for regret; the deed had been done. It had cost her much, but perhaps the sacrifice would somehow be redeemed at a worthwhile price in the life of her beloved Jacob.

In the midst of the hushed tones within the palace walls, Bathsheba was acutely aware of one reverberating sound— the beating of her own heart. David, her beloved David, was dying, and she could do nothing about it. Although he was larger than life in her eyes, she understood that even this man who had been a loving husband must go the way of all the earth and return to his Maker. The end was not clearly known to Bathsheba, but there was one thing that she could do something about. She could secure her son's inheritance. He would be king. David had promised her this. But now, among the shuffle of David's illness and Adonijah's self-proclaimed takeover, the promise had been lost, kicked underfoot by the adjustment to transition.

As Bathsheba made her way to her dying husband's room, the words of Nathan the prophet resounded in her ears. This man whose words always before led to life, whether by blatant correction or encouragement, had come with the passion of God burning in his eyes, prompting her to put her husband in remembrance of his vow. It was her job to turn the heart of this father toward his son, even as she had turned the heart of her son toward his father. This was not merely an act of self-preservation. It was her duty as Solomon's mother to insure his position in the hallowed halls of God's proclaimed destiny for them all. And so she went with purpose being birthed in every step she took. Bowing low before her king, she made her petition known in response to his query concerning the desire of her heart: "Give your son his rightful place." This affirmation must come by his order alone. She yielded the fate of herself and her son into his hands, and David rose to the occasion, crowning Solomon king according to his promise and the ordinance of God. As David breathed his last breath he rested well, knowing all was in order. To his dying day, the heart of his wife and his son had the security of his covering. He left parting words of wisdom that echoed in Solomon's spirit, always tugging on the fringes of his robe when he strayed, calling him back home, back to the arms of God.

Through the Fire, to the Limit, to the Wall

The intensity of a mother's love, whether animal or human, is legendary. The stories of things mothers have done in the name of preserving their offspring have been written among the chronicles of unforgettable stories. Nobody messes with a mother's love. She is deeply nurturing, fiercely protective, unabashedly uninhibited when it comes to doing whatever must be done to ensure the welfare of her children. And well she should, for this was part of God's original design. Woven into the fiber of every mother's spirit is the instinct to protect the precious charges He has placed in her care. As we study the mothers of the Bible, the ordained calling of every mother becomes crystal-clear. Mothers are purveyors of life, created to give it, nurture it, protect it, and release it at the appropriate time to fulfill the purposes of God. I would dare to say that the role of a mother is so intensely powerful that the destinies of nations lie in her hands.

Small wonder that woman is such a dangerous foe in the mind of Satan! The enemy works overtime to distort and destroy the very spirit of motherhood among women today. From the beginning he waged war against her and her off-spring. As time is winding down, his hatred has come to a boil, causing him to pull out all the stops in order to destroy our children.

> "The king of Egypt said to the Hebrew midwives, whose names were Shiphrah and Puah; 'When you help the Hebrew women in childbirth and observe them on the delivery stool, if it is a boy, kill him; but if it is a girl, let her live'" (Exodus 1:15,16 NIV).

> "Then Herod, when he saw that he was deceived by the wise men, was exceedingly angry; and he sent forth and put to death all the male children who were in Bethlehem and in all its districts, from two

years old and under, according to the time which he had determined from the wise men" (Matthew 2:16,17 NKJV).

"The dragon stood in front of the woman who was about to give birth, so that he might devour her child the moment it was born" (Revelation 12:4 NIV).

For those of you who are stymied by the symbolism in the book of Revelation, this portion of Scripture prophetically outlines both the birth of Christ and the twelve tribes of Israel, whose offspring would then be all believers. From the book of Genesis, when God informed the serpent that there would be one born who would destroy his authority over men, Satan has been on the rampage, seeking to exterminate the life of any child who might be a threat to his kingdom. Down through the ages he sought to be one step ahead of Jesus Christ, to cut Him off before He grew to fulfill His purpose, the salvation of mankind. From Genesis to Revelation to present day the spirit of assassination has been released against children. For even though Christ was born, died, rose, and will come again, the quest is on to extinguish our modern-day messiahs—messiahs in the sense of those whom God has chosen to use daily to administer healing, deliverance, and restoration in our homes, neighborhoods, cities, and nations.

The war against "women birthin' babies" has not stopped. Why? Because whether they are conceived on purpose or "by mistake," God has a purpose for every life. Satan is privy to the discussions held in heaven concerning God's plans toward us, and his mission is still to circumvent God's agenda from being fulfilled as often as possible. No woman knows what her child will become unless she is told by the Lord, but the heavens know. I believe that God honors those who fight to preserve the life of their children in the face of very real obstacles by making a way out of no way for them. God's agenda must prevail despite the questions and fears that rise in the face of an unexpected pregnancy, the absence of a father, the financial lack, the fear of the future, attacks without and within, disturbing medical innuendoes, the limited means of support materially or emotionally, the interrupted personal or professional agendas...the "inconvenience" of it all, according to individual personal circumstance.

> "For those God foreknew he also predestined to be conformed to the likeness of his Son....And those he predestined, he also called..." (Romans 8:29,30 NIV).

> "For he chose us in him before the creation of the world to be holy and blameless in his sight" (Ephesians 1:4 NIV).

> "In him we were also chosen, having been predestined according to the plan of him who works out everything in conformity with the purpose of his will..." (Ephesians 1:11 NIV).

In essence, before any of us existed, God's plan existed. According to His foreknowledge of our personal dispositions, He was able to know which tasks to designate to whom in order to effectively carry out His purpose. We—you and I—are merely the clothes wrapped around the various purposes of God. You are here *on purpose!* And no matter how you feel right now, you do have a purpose. You will know if you are fulfilling that purpose or not by the level of fulfillment you feel. People who are walking in their purpose are excited about life. Those who are not spend their time wondering what they're supposed to be doing with themselves or searching for a partner or some other type of outward stimuli to fill the empty space they feel. If you fall into this category, ask God to reveal your personal purpose to you.

The hints lie in what you longed to be when you were a little girl, before practicality set in. Your dreams usually coincide with your gifts. Your gifts are the things that come easily to you. Others rejoice in them, but they seem like no big deal to you because they are a natural outflow of your God-given abilities and personality. Ask God how you can use them to bless others, then watch yourself get pulled into the flow of God's purpose for you. This is the place of true fulfillment, peace, and abundant joy. Why? Because you are finally doing what you were created to do. This is what the dragon wants to snuff out. If it were up to him, none of us would be born to even discover our purpose, much less fulfill it. So the enemy stands with his mouth open, waiting to devour the purpose of God from being birthed in our lives.

Yes, the spirit of assassination is still alive and well, cleverly cloaked beneath the deceptive disguise of abortion. Please keep in mind that this is not meant to cause you to fall into condemnation if you have had an abortion. Rather, it is an attempt to expose the lie of the enemy. We get in trouble and fall prey to error when we lack knowledge. Once we come into the light and confess our sin, God is faithful to forgive us. However, it behooves us to know exactly what is at work here. It is not the life of the child that Satan is after. It is the purpose of God that is within that child. Satan wants to abort the purposes of God from ever coming to pass. We are the living, breathing, moving purposes of God. Your children, your future children, and your children's children are the embodiment of God's purposes. Small wonder Satan wants them dead. People fulfilling the purposes of God—that's just too much power walking around on the earth, and it can only spell trouble for him. And you thought abortion was just some idea modern-day women came up with to fix an "inconvenient" circumstance!

Whose Body Is It, Anyway?

I sadly shake my head every time the abortion debate begins. The argument that women should have the "right" to do what they want with their own bodies sounds reasonable enough, until you stop to consider a deeper truth—none of our bodies really belong to us. Not a woman's, not a man's. Every body belongs to the Lord. He purchased them all.

> "The body is not meant for sexual immorality, but for the Lord, and the Lord for the body" (1 Corinthians 6:13 NIV).

> "Do you not know that your bodies are members of Christ himself?" (1 Corinthians 6:15 NIV).

> "Do you not know that your body is a temple of the Holy Spirit, who is in you, whom you have received from God? You are not your own; you were bought at a price. Therefore honor God with your body" (1 Corinthians 6:19,20 NIV).

> "You were bought at a price; do not become slaves of men. Brothers [sisters], each man [or woman], as responsible to God, should remain in the situation God called him [or her] to" (1 Corinthians 7:23,24 NIV).

"For every living soul belongs to me, the father [or mother] as well as the son [or daughter]—both alike belong to me" (Ezekiel 18:4 NIV).

"Therefore, I urge you, brothers [sisters], in view of God's mercy, to offer your bodies as living sacrifices, holy and pleasing to God—this is your spiritual act of worship. Do not conform any longer to the pattern of this world, but be transformed by the renewing of your mind. Then you will be able to test and approve what God's will is—his good, pleasing and perfect will" (Romans 12:1,2 NIV).

So much for our "rights." Our "rights" are now hidden in Christ. Our "rights" should now be exercised for God's glory instead of for our own personal agendas. Our "rights" now pertain to spiritual authority, not a natural reign over others or ourselves. We are all called to submit to God right now. This is not bondage, for God has called us into the light of His Spirit. And where His Spirit is, there is liberty (2 Corinthians 3:17). Broken down to street terms, you obey the rules, you're a free woman. You break the rules, you go to jail. Jail is bondage—anything you can't break out of, plain and simple. You don't know what true bondage is until you've been forced to remain in one spot. God has given you plenty of room in which to move around within the confines of His protective instructions. When you choose to venture beyond the boundaries He so lovingly set, the dragon waits to bind you and devour you, as well as your children.

A Woman's Work Is Never Done

As most mothers know, the real work begins after childbirth and doesn't get any easier from there. Raising children in today's society is harder than ever. As time winds down and the enemy of our souls watches the last grains of his destructive chances sift through eternity's hourglass, his campaign against the purposes of God, which are wrapped in your children, intensifies. The dragon did not cash in his chips when you slid past the first phase of his evil campaign. He just deceitfully wrapped up the spirit of abortion in other forms of disguise—abuse, neglect, lack of discipline, gangs, drugs, broken homes...anything that will assist him in snuffing out that child's desire to rise to the occasion of fulfilling his or her purpose. The good news here? The battle has already been won through Christ Jesus!

It is important not to take your difficulties with your children personally but to instead attack them spiritually. The Word of God clearly states that the dragon is outraged at the woman and is on the warpath against her children. Mothers and their children are attacked without and within. Mothers fail to see their own value, while children have lost all sense of hope for the future. Most expect to die early, or at least give up, and have resigned themselves to this ill-imagined fate.

"I'm just a mother," or "I'm just a housewife," I have heard many a woman utter. I'm always quite incredulous upon hearing this comment. I used to think to myself, "How could they ever put the word "just" before that job description?" Then I realized that society, fueled by the invisible dragon, has done a pretty good job of making the role of homemaker and mother extremely unglamorous. As a matter of fact, these roles have been stripped of all their honor. Well, I'm here to put it back. I'm going to put it back through giving you a new understanding. Although I daresay some of you are already getting it because more and more women are leaving the workforce and migrating back to their homes, reclaiming their children and their households. Those who once held "Leave It to Beaver" days in scornful regard are now admitting there is something to be said for being at home when the children return from school.

What is the purpose of a mother? It goes beyond bringing a child into the world or the personal satisfaction you get from looking at that cute little face full of love and dependence on you and only you. It's more than how sweet they smell, and how they hold their arms out to you when they attempt their first step. It's even more than the day your little girl becomes a woman and you teach her what that means or the first day your son's voice begins to drop. And yes, it's more than your child's first urge to cry, "Mama!" at the first pang of fear or the exultant cry of victory. It's so high above, so far beyond, so much greater than you. Your role as a mother affects destiny beyond your personal space or home. It was a mother who raised Thomas Edison to give light to the world. It was a mother who raised Mahatma Gandhi to change a nation. It was a mother who raised Harriet Tubman to lead slaves to freedom. It was a mother who raised Jesus Christ to die for the sins of the world. Don't you think God did a character study before selecting the mother for His only begotten Son? Every woman in Israel longed to give birth to the Messiah, and after careful consideration, God moved after His own counsel and chose Mary. Mary was the woman God decided He could trust to give life to His Son. To nurture Him naturally and spiritually. To teach Him obedience. To release Him into His purpose. It was Mary who encouraged Jesus to perform His first miracle. Even Jesus, who was God incarnate, yielded to the influence of His earthly mother.

I find it interesting to note that throughout the Bible, mothers are mentioned more than fathers in references about children. I think this is deliberate. In God's design, it is a mother who teaches and grooms a child. The father is the enforcer of what she has taught. For those who are struggling

---

It is a mother who is usually most spiritually attuned to the possibilities within her child. And she can nurture them like no other, gently planting seeds in that child's spirit and watering them with motherly encouragement as the years go by until one day they bear precious fruit.

---

to raise children in a home where the father is absent, this should be an encouragement to you. God has equipped you to have everything you need to raise your child. He, God Himself, will step in to fill that missing man's shoes and enforce what you have instilled. He is a Father to the fatherless. He has your back! Many mothers feel they have to be both mother and father to their children. Not true. Continue to be a mother, continue to be a woman. Be fierce only in prayer, warring on your knees for your children when the enemy of their souls comes against them with bad influences, dangerous opportunities, and invitations to rebel. Be unbending only in the face of disappointment, knowing God is able to keep you and yours no matter how hard the struggle. Be courageous fighting the good fight, standing anyway when you grow weary of standing for what is right while everything around you contradicts your faith. Stand and see God fill in the gaps for you, because mothers are dear to the heart of God. He knows the way they take and all that they go through. He equips them to bear the pain of the sword that eventually pierces the heart of every mother, regardless of domestic circumstance, even as it pierced the heart of Mary, the mother of His own Son. Yet He has selected woman for the awesome privilege of being a mother.

That's What Mothers Are Made Of

It is a mother who will live and die and fight for the life of her child. In the fourth chapter of 2 Kings, Elisha prayed for the barren Shunammite woman to have a son. After several years the son became ill while out in the fields with his father. The father sent him home to his mother, where he sat on her lap and died. She then laid him on his bed and, without telling anyone what had happened, went to find the prophet. When asked if anything was wrong, she said, "All is well." She would not even confess the death of her son. Yet she refused to leave the prophet until he agreed to go with her. Elisha then went with her and brought the boy back to life. A mother will stand against the odds when everyone else declares that the life of her child is beyond hope. It is her faith that will bring a dead soul back to life.

It is a mother who is usually most spiritually attuned to the possibilities within her child. And she can nurture them like no other, gently planting seeds in that child's spirit and watering them with motherly encouragement as the years go by until one day they bear precious fruit.

Jochebed, the mother of Moses, sensed that there was something unique about her son. Though she would rather keep him with her, she sacrificed her hold on him for the greater cause. Yet she was given the privilege of nursing him, and he never forgot who he was. He went on to become the deliverer of a nation. Hannah, who spent many years grieving because she was barren, cried out to the Lord for a child. After finally bearing a son, she gave him up to the ser- vice of the Lord. Her yearly visits to him were a time of lov- ingly reminding him what a special child he was, how she had prayed for him, and how she knew that God was going to do great things in his life. This son, Samuel, grew up to be a judge, prophet, and priest over Israel. He crowned the first two kings of Israel and literally led the nation through his- toric transition. He ended up with two books of the Bible named after him. All of this happened because a mother was spiritually sensitive and set her son on the right path to ful- filling his God-ordained purpose. God, in turn, blessed Hannah with five additional children to reward her for her relinquishment.

On the other hand, there is Samson. I have often ques- tioned what happened to him. His mother, who remains nameless in Scripture, was also barren well into her years. And though an angel of the Lord told her her son's purpose and his father asked the angel for specific instructions on how to raise their child, discipline and a sense of purpose did not ever seem to be instilled in Samson. When reading this story, I always thought to myself that if that had happened to me, the boy would have gotten sick and tired of me nursing and rehearsing that story to him. He would definitely have known his purpose by the time I was finished with him! Perhaps the joy of finally having a child after wanting one for so long made Samson's mother and father lax in their training and instruction. When Samson started to err in the decisions of his life, their weak protests (which I noted did not include a reminder of his purpose) were met with his blatant disregard for their authority. His lack of honor and disobedience toward them most certainly led to his early death.

Though the mother of every wayward child cannot be faulted for her offspring's ethical or moral decline, she can certainly cling to the comfort that she put everything into that child she was called to deposit—spiritually, emotionally, and physically. If she has done that and continues to labor in prayer for her child, then she has a solid promise from God on which she can stand. That child will be back.

> "Train a child in the way he should go, and when he
> is old he will not turn from it" (Proverbs 22:6 NIV).

It is a mother who, through the example of yielding to God and to the head of her household, teaches a child the spirit of submission to God and to authority. If she is rebellious and hard herself, her children will follow her example to their ruin.

Take the example of Jezebel, whom we will examine even further in a later chapter. For now, we will concentrate on her mothering skills. Jezebel controlled her husband as well as 850 priests. She had an innocent civilian killed in order to placate her pouting husband, threatened Elijah, the man of God, and disdainfully confronted the next king of Israel before falling to her death. She was just plain ole evil. She got her way, regardless of how it hurt anyone else, and she obviously had little regard or respect for men. This was the legacy she passed on to her sons, Ahaziah, who lasted all of two years as king, and Joram, who led the country into war and famine. Finally, after God had had enough of this family's evil ways, He took the kingdom from them. So Jezebel raised her sons to lose their legacy. She got what she wanted, died, and left behind no good thing for generations to remember.

Meanwhile, Jezebel also had a daughter, Athaliah, who married Jehoram, the king of Judah. Athaliah was truly her mother's daughter. She exhibited an identical character trait—that of being a control freak. Athaliah carried on the tradition of her mother, Jezebel, influencing her husband to walk in the ways of the house of Ahab—worshiping idols, leading the people astray, and eventually killing all of his own brothers. Her youngest son, Ahaziah, went on to become king after her husband died, and she seemed fine with that. The Bible says that she encouraged her son in doing wrong. There you have it. She was still running things—keeping tight apron strings attached to her baby boy. When he got killed in battle, this evil woman rose up to kill all of her grandchildren so that she could remain queen! One of her husband's daughters by another one of his wives, Jehosheba, who was married to the high priest (and was obviously in tune with the purposes of God), managed to hide one of Ahaziah's sons until he was of age to take the throne, and then Athaliah was executed. She was murdered as her mother was murdered. The end of rebelling and circumventing authority is always death.

Looking at the spiritual message in this story, it is important to be able to translate these lessons to address where we presently live. We all have met, seen, or known personally the domineering mother, especially when we deal with her sons. Many a wife shares horror stories of being married to a man who is still controlled by his mother and the havoc it is wreaking on her marriage. There is a difference between giving honor to your mother and being controlled by her. One is respectful reverence that gives life to all you do, and the other is debilitating and paralyzing, stunting progress in every area of your life. Many mothers become dangerously attached to their sons, replacing their mate with their son. Their own search for the praises of men and for the love and fulfillment they fail to receive from their mate propels them to enter into emasculating relationships with their sons. This is out of God's order. Sons are not created to fill the void that you've determined your mate won't fill. Children are not made to be bargaining tools and instruments of manipulation to retaliate against, insult, draw, bind, or repel the man in your life.

Neither are they toys to be coddled for your own personal enjoyment. They are little people who come laden with purpose and endless possibilities that must not be distorted through overindulgence. Remember, Rebekah lost her son when she hoarded his affections and caused him to deceive his own father. Though her intention was good (to secure the blessing on his life in accordance with God's prophetic word), her modus operandi was wrong and it cost her the joy of being able to see her son as she lived out the rest of her years. That which she had so tightly held slipped through her fingers, much to her dismay. She spoiled Jacob and taught him to be a trickster used to having his way, which set him up for a difficult future until he was broken in a wrestling match with God. This is not what God had in mind when he granted women the gift of influence.

Mothers are called to raise "men and women of God." How do they do that? By being living testaments, consistent examples of the type of person they would like their children to become. By speaking wisdom into their children's lives after the manner of the Proverbs. By grooming their children spiritually, emotionally, and physically. By helping their children tap into the boundless possibilities within themselves because of the power of God at work within them. By being like Jesus in the house—taking on the role of mediator. By turning the hearts of the father and the son, the father and the daughter, toward one another (Malachi 4:6) so that the boy gets the male affirmation he needs in order to be a man and so that the girl grows up affirmed as a woman, knowing she deserves to be loved properly. This enables a son to "leave and cleave" (Genesis 2:24). This enables a daughter to grasp the concept of walking in oneness with her husband. This builds solid men and women who fulfill their purpose and further the world's destiny.

Wisdom Is a Woman

Although Bathsheba and David didn't get off to what one would call a good start, they obviously got on track somewhere along the way. I find it interesting that when Solomon recorded the things he had been taught as a boy, he gave a very balanced delivery, encouraging his son to listen to the counsel of both his father and his mother. It seems that both

David and Bathsheba were equally active in grooming their son to be king. He was obviously impressed with the example his mother set before him because he chose to personify wisdom as a woman. What an honor to her credit! He was affirmed by her motherly love and tender sharing of wise truths and by his father's clear instructions. But he was also affirmed in the love he saw pass between his mother and father. It was his security, but it was also his most profound lesson. It was a living example to him of God's divine order. Of respect and partnership. Of the equal value of his mother and his father. Of the need for both the head and the heart to work together to orchestrate all things to their highest good. Both were needed.

> "For I was my father's son, tender and only beloved in the sight of my mother" (Proverbs 4:3 KJV).

> "My son, hear the instruction of thy father, and forsake not the law of thy mother" (Proverbs 1:8 KJV).

> "My son, keep thy father's commandment, and forsake not the law of thy mother" (Proverbs 6:20 KJV).

> "A wise son maketh a glad father: but a foolish man despiseth his mother" (Proverbs 15:20 KJV).

> "Hearken unto thy father that begat thee, and despise not thy mother when she is old" (Proverbs 23:22 KJV).

Bathsheba knew what Jochebed, Moses' mother; Hannah, Samuel's mother; and Mary, the mother of Jesus, all understood as well. Their children were not theirs to keep. They were simply on loan from the throne of God to be raised in a manner that would prepare them to change the course of history, the lives of many, and the conclusion of eternity. Husbands are "to have and to hold," children are to be groomed and released.

If I were asked to write a chapter of proverbs for mothers, I believe it would go something like this:

> Who can find a virtuous mother? There are many, yet her price is far beyond riches untold. She preserves the lives of her children beneath the covering of strong wings that are lined with tenderness. Her breasts comfort and nourish hungry spirits. Her hands soothe away disappointed tears. Her arms shield her children from all they fear. Her tongue is filled with life and affirmation, profound truths, wise observations, and uncompromising correction. She is fierce and courageous, standing against any assaults the enemy brings against her charges. She is inventive in times of lack. Industrious still in times of weariness. She stands even when she feels she can stand no longer. She is a living, godly example of submission before her children. She turns the hearts of her children toward their father, both heavenly and earthly. She covers her house in prayer, keeping vigilant watch over the purposes of God coming to fruition in her children. She wars for their "blessing" in intercession. She secures their inheritance by setting them on a sound path paved with godly values. She prepares her children for the world at large and instructs them in the ways of integrity, love, and giving. She maintains her femininity in the midst of seemingly masculine circumstances. She is celebrated within her walls. Her inheritance is great, for she affects the lives of her children's children. She leaves a legacy of honor for them to follow. She is a

woman *of* purpose. She is a woman on purpose. She celebrates God. She celebrates her children. She celebrates the cycle of life, the season of embracing, the season of release, for her confidence is not in the arm of flesh, but in her Maker, and in that knowledge she draws her comfort and sustains her peace.

What is the role of a mother? To preserve the life of her children. To keep them from being devoured by the dragon. To nurture purpose. To blow on the embers of those little spirits until their hands reach up to God. To secure the blessing. To guard their inheritance. To release them into becoming pillars of destiny. This is where the honor is found. There is no such thing as being "just a mother" because motherhood is a precious assignment from God. It has its season. And in that season, enjoy the identity of being a Mother. Capitalized on purpose. Because God chose you on purpose for such a time as this.

> "And Adam called his wife's name Eve; because she was the mother of all the living" (Genesis 3:20 KJV).

Dear Heavenly Father, thank You for the gift of my child. I am humbled that You thought me worthy of watching over someone who is so precious to You. Equip me with all the wisdom, strength, and insight that I need to complete my assignment in a way that will be pleasing to You. Show me the way that I should take even as I instruct this one who You have entrusted into my care. As I commit him (her) into Your care, I trust You to keep him (her) safe in all of his (her) ways. Grant me an increased sense of discernment to recognize the work of the enemy in my child's life. Give me the strength to battle against the forces that will seek to pull his (her) heart away from You, to break his (her) spirit and bend his (her) will. When I grow weary, strengthen my weary arms and renew my faith in Your ability to keep us all. By the authority that You've given me over the life of my child, through Christ, I abort the plans of the enemy and his agenda for destroying the purposes of God in my child. Guide my prayer life to strategically call forth the destiny of this little one. Help me to secure the inheritance that You have reserved for him (her). But most of all, Lord, in those times when the going gets tough, remind me that children are only part of my reward for answering Your call. Reaffirm my worth when the world is telling me I have no value, and let me find my validation and all that is truly worthwhile in You. In Jesus' name. Amen.

FIVE

It's a Sister Thing

*L*ittle pudgy fingers
full of wonder
        pressed against unfamiliar lips
                to see if her miniature visitor too
                        was warm
        fingers equally inquisitive
        and full of questions
                reached back
                reaching out to entwine themselves
                        in locks of hair not her own
                                to see...oh, just to see
                such is the way of babes
                        bearing no preconceived notions
                                no learned cautions as yet
                they simply trust
                        and embrace
        their first mutual giggle
                becoming a covenant
a covenant to friendship and sisterhood
        and as the years struggled to keep up with their height
                their blossoming
                their unfolding into young women
        the seasons changed as subtly
as the revelation
        of who they were came to light
                in the lines
                        reflected in their mirrors
        these two women
                who shared everything
                        from lollipops
                to lipstick

now found that men
were more precious than toys
and lines of permissible intimacy were silently drawn
in the dawning of the understanding
that some things just couldn't be shared...
pain, yes
laughter, yes
discouragement, yes
an outfit, yes
men?...no!
absolutely not!
and the bridge was damaged
leaving gutters and trenches
that made friendship harder to cross
sisterhood more difficult to reach
and trust
woman to woman
an elusive treasure
and two little girls
now dressed in women's clothing
longed for a time they once knew
when they shared and shared alike
when there were no secrets between them
for they were all told under the covers
after bedtime stories and goodnight kisses
when they were closer than close
tighter than tight
thicker than blood
true blue
friends
and sisters...

*O*ooh, that looks lovely on you. You should get it!" my admirer told me. It was 7:30 A.M. and my favorite store was having a knock-down-drag-out sale. Eighty percent off of everything! Oooh, mama, I was in my glory! And so were my sisters—women I had never seen before in my life, but this morning we were bonding big-time. Compliments were flying. Words of advice were being dispersed. "Mmm, it's pretty, but you looked slimmer in the other outfit." "That color is very becoming." "You really think so?" "Oh, yes, but then again, everything you've tried on looks good on you." Of course, there's always one in the bunch, holding her breath, hoping you won't like what you've tried on so that she can scoop it up as soon as you've discarded it. After all, one woman's trash is another woman's treasure. But as I headed back to my dressing room, I thought to myself, *If only women could treat one another this way all the time.* In that crowd there were no masks. Several women hadn't even bothered to try to put on makeup at this ridiculous hour. (Can you tell I'm not a morning person?) No pretenses. We were one, all on the same mission—to secure as many bargains as we could.

Every woman's coup was to be celebrated. Everyone was soft and warm, giggling and twirling in front of the mirror, nurturing one another to look the best we could, uplifting one another, pointing out each other's best assets...women being women, and there wasn't a man present!

So where does this image of catty women come from? From that ole serpent, that's who. Who else knows better the fact that a house divided against itself will not stand? The curse in the garden, the one that woman would have this overwhelming desire toward man, also gave birth to the notion of competition between women. We became one another's greatest threat to what each of us really wanted— the heart of man. Amazingly early we begin to compare notes. Hmm, let's see, who's got prettier hair, prettier eyes, a better figure? I was excused from this process all the way through school because I was a late bloomer. Being overlooked actually gave me the vantage point to scope out some very interesting things I might have missed had I been a part of the mad dash to have a "man" in junior high school.

Every day after school, two girls would meet to fight over "their man." Every day the story was the same. The young man who was the focal point of the dispute would not be present, and inevitably within three days you would see him walking around with a completely different girl! I was quite befuddled at this phenomenon at first, but later concluded that no man was worth me scuffing up my shoes and ruining an outfit. Neither would I ever become angry with another female over a man. It was clear to me, even back then, that it was the man who made the choice. My second vow, made at the wise age of 11, was that I would not be party to the philandering of any man. I came to the conclusion that we as women assist men in their waywardness when we accommodate their infidelities.

Share and Share Alike?

It all began at such a tender age—the realization that man was a hot commodity. Already the young women around me had to decide if they would be willing to share or not. And the young men were having a good time. They all felt like celebrities, choosing each week who they would flatter with their much-sought-after affections. Partners switched at regular intervals as the more popular young men made their rounds. And fast friends became quick enemies in the fallout. After all, why should the brothers honor our friendships if we weren't willing to guard them? For those who had pride, this meant war, and may the better woman win. But there was another contingency—these young woman were happy to get whatever attention they could. They had already decided that something was better than nothing at all. And so they resigned themselves to their designated day and vowed to make the best of it.

I was mortified to find myself in the middle of such triangles as I listened to my friends relay information about their so-called "relationships." My greatest challenge was remembering who not to mention to whom. I certainly did not want to be responsible for any trouble. At the ages of 13 and 14, these girls were already hardened. It showed in their faces, in their body language. As I was ahead of my age group in school, and therefore behind my peers in years and development, I was not allowed to even *think* about talking to a boy yet. But I was drawing some pretty well-defined summaries

about this whole man/woman thing from all of my obser-
vances.

The young women who knowingly "shared" their
boyfriends seemed to walk around with a cloud hanging over
their heads. Their ability to excel in school, as well as their
self-esteem, were low. They exchanged the pride of "having
a man" for taking pride in themselves. They were cynical
about life already, not expecting much of anything. They had
already summed up that it was in the nature of men to mess
around. "Men are just that way," was already a popular catch
phrase. The lot these girls had already assigned themselves
was too much to bear, yet that was life. They ended up
having children at an early age with these men. In most
cases, both girls would be pregnant by the same man at the
same time. The disgrace they hoped to avoid by having a
man had brought them even deeper embarrassment with
unending responsibility. All of this I watched from the sidelines, safe within the circumference of my mother and
father's strict rules, jaw dropped, eyebrows to scalp with my
hair standing on end. I vowed that no man was ever going to
even kiss me until my wedding night. Between my fear of
God and my mother, my mother being first in this equation,
that was enough to keep me centered on purity until I navi-
gated my way through high school. Might I add that none of
these young ladies ever got married to these young men.
They all grew up and went their separate ways with bad tastes
in their mouths, beginning a generation of children grown
distant from their fathers from the experience.

Since high school the marker seems to have gone up on
the "sharing" phenomenon. Now this is a familiar topic on
every talk show. Women and men, almost lackadaisical in
posture, introduce one another to the "other person" they

are seeing, while stating that they're willing to share if everyone else is game. Perhaps it is a sign of the age.

> "In that day seven women will take hold of one man and say, 'We will eat our own food and provide our own clothes; only let us be called by your name. Take away our disgrace!'" (Isaiah 4:1 NIV).

I am fascinated that we, as human beings who are essentially selfish in nature, could ever sink to such a level of forfeiture. That is exactly what it is. It is cheapening God's creation, namely yourself, and selling out for less than what He desires you to have. In the nineteenth chapter of Genesis, Lot's daughters decided to "share" their father after they escaped from Sodom and Gomorrah in order to preserve their family lineage. So they got him drunk and took turns sleeping with him. They both became pregnant and gave birth to Moab and Ammon. They gave birth to two nations that became two of the greatest enemies of Israel, nations that remained a perpetual thorn in their sides. "Sharing" a man gives birth to things in your life that will afflict you long-term—emotionally, spiritually, and let's not forget physically. It is a dangerous time not to be pure as diseases run rampant between multiple partners both in and out of the church.

God has called us to be "well-kept women" who know our value. He has fashioned us to be "one" with *one* man, and vice versa. Anything else is a destructive blow against our spirits and how we were made. Our spirits were not made to accommodate anything outside of God's original design. We should protect ourselves and protect one another. We do ourselves and our sisters a great disservice when we assist men in mistreating us. We collectively get to set the standard on how men treat us by the respect we render to one another. It is time to be honest and admit that in most cases of strife between women, one can usually find a man at the center. Time-out for this! The energy we waste on women who we perceive as threats to the life of our relationships would be better spent leveling a convicting conversation at a brother who has dared to consider cheapening a sister.

The Other Woman

Something I have often wondered is where was the man who was caught with the adulterous woman? The text in John chapter eight says that she was "caught in the act," so where was the man? Why was she the only one dragged before Jesus for judgment? Didn't the law in Leviticus state that if a man and woman were caught in adultery, *both* the adulterer *and* the adulteress were to be put to death? But there they all were, back in the garden with Adam, pointing their finger at "that woman" with no mention of the man who was involved with her in sin. They were setting her up to be stoned while her partner walked. Think about it!

We are no better today. As scandal has rocked our nation's leadership in the past year, I heard disparaging remarks from men and women alike leveled at the young woman involved. I was shocked at the cruelty of women as they condemned this young lady without ever mentioning her partner. Our leader was dismissed as "having a problem," therefore, there was no need to waste much conversation on him. He should be left alone to run the affairs of the country before it affected our purses. But "that woman"! There was plenty to say about her!

I was always a bit confused as to why everyone treated the "other woman" as if she were the criminal when the affair was discovered. Try as I might, I couldn't quite get the image of this horrible woman in red violently twisting the arm of this poor, helpless man and forcing him to have an affair with her. Let's face it, no matter how hard she flirts, it is the man

---

ow does a woman give away a man? By giving him what she thinks he needs instead of what he says he wants. This is why it is of utmost importance to listen to your man.

---

who ultimately makes the decision to go for it. As I grew up and began to experience all the ins and outs of romance, I stumbled across the reason for this sort of behavior when I found myself replaced by the "other woman." After the first blow, I recall my reaction being, "But what's wrong with me?" With that being too painful a question, it was easier to turn an accusing finger at "that woman." It was all her fault! After all, my man was perfect. He didn't make foolish choices.

Why I couldn't simply conclude that the young man in this situation lacked integrity or was an idiot to choose someone other than myself is beyond me. Perhaps I was too besotted at the time to think him a fool even though he had hurt me deeply. All I know is that it was quite cathartic to place the blame on "her" shoulders. It was just too overwhelming to actually take an honest assessment of how I could have contributed to the demise of my own relationship. And so the "other woman" earned the scarlet letter, thus purging me of all guilt, freeing me from examining my own shortcomings.

As I continued my exodus through the land of romantic relationships, certain revelations began to unfold. Men seemed to fall into two categories when it came to this "other woman" issue. One group of men had unfaithful spirits. It was just in them to wander, and not only when it came to women. They were unfaithful in every area of life. They found it difficult to remain committed to anything over a long period of time. These were the restless, prone to roam whenever it began to take any amount of work to maintain what they had started. The second group of men were those with more of a fixed temperament. "Don't rock the boat" was their philosophy. They liked routine, no sudden changes, no confrontations. Only long-term misery could remove them from their perches. These were the men who women gave away. It's true that no woman "takes" a man from a woman. She gives him away. I can hear the screams of indignation all the way in Chicago as you read this, but hear me out. How does a woman give away a man? By giving him what she *thinks* he *needs* instead of what he *says* he *wants*. This is why it is of utmost importance to listen to your man.

And, ladies, men mean exactly what they say. Yes means yes, no means no, and I don't like that means I don't like that. They are not like us, where no means no for now and is subject to change. Or I want this, but if I can't have it I'll adjust. Unfortunately, for everything you won't do for your man, there is a woman waiting in the wings who is perfectly ready and willing to accommodate his unmet desires. And what does any starving person do when food is placed in front of him? He eats.

Betty Wright sang a popular song back in the late sixties entitled, "The Cleanup Woman." She sang the song from the vantage point of the wife who had made it easy for the cleanup woman to take all the love she left behind—she felt she should warn other wives not to make the same mistake. When asked in a Barbara Walters interview about how she dealt with her husband's infidelities, Lady Bird Johnson said, "If all those ladies had some good points that I didn't have, I hope I had the sense to learn by it" (*People* magazine, February 15, 1999). Perhaps she had stumbled across the same discovery. Now, this is not a justification for unfaithfulness. No excuse is acceptable. However, in order to beat the enemy, you have to know how the enemy plays. The serpent Adam and Eve interacted with in the garden is still on the rampage, seeking to divide and conquer. He hates marriage and will stop at nothing to destroy it. If he can wreak havoc in a household, he can short-circuit the purposes of God being birthed or growing to fruition.

How subtle he was to whisper in Sarah's ear that God was not capable of giving her husband, Abraham, a child from her body. Abraham was content to wait on God, but Sarah had to take control of the situation.

"So after Abram had been living in Canaan ten years, Sarai his wife took her Egyptian maidservant

Hagar and gave her to her husband to be his wife. He slept with Hagar, and she conceived. When she knew she was pregnant, she began to despise her mistress. Then Sarai said to Abram, 'You are responsible for the wrong I am suffering. I put my servant in your arms, and now that she knows she is pregnant, she despises me'" (Genesis 16:3-5 NIV).

She gave her maid Hagar to Abraham and instructed him to sleep with her. Hagar became pregnant with Abraham's child and that's when peace and harmony made a hasty retreat from their dwelling place. Now Hagar had something Sarah wanted, and Hagar knew it. Sarah knew it, too. All her years of being a treasured wife were rocked off their axle by insecurity. She became irritable and difficult to be around, and you better believe that everyone got a taste of her caustic rancor. Poor Abraham was stuck in the middle. He loved his wife, but now he was bound to Hagar, too, because she bore his child. Still, there was no way that he was going to take Hagar's side. After all, she was the other woman; his first loyalty was to his wife. And so he left the two women to work it out on their own. His only response to Sarah's complaints about Hagar's attitude was, "Hey, you handle it in the way you see fit." Smart man. So Sarah let Hagar have it. It became so unbearable for Hagar that she was willing to leave the comfort of where she was, even in her pregnant state, to brave the unknown. The angel of the Lord had to tell her to pull herself together, go back home, and submit to Sarah.

Eventually, after Hagar's baby was born, Sarah finally had a baby of her own. Now they were back to playing on a level field. Sarah found no need to keep Hagar around to dip into the pie and take away any portion of her son's inheritance, so at the first sign of trouble between the two children, Hagar was dismissed and sent on her way. Such is the eventual painful fate of the "other woman." This is where the deception should end. The "other woman" rarely gets her man. And when she does, it opens the door to a whole different flavor of pain.

Take the example of Rachel and Leah. Jacob was deeply in love with Rachel, working seven years in order to have her hand in marriage. On Jacob's wedding night, Rachel's father switched Rachel for Leah. Poor Jacob, not being willing to give up on Rachel, worked another seven years for her hand as well. This left Leah, though married to Jacob, always on the outside looking in on her own marriage. She spent all of her days trying to win the heart of a man who never wanted her. No matter how many children Leah bore him, Jacob's heart remained with Rachel. The part of this story that always befuddled me was why Leah felt entitled to Jacob's love. After all, she got him by default in the first place. When her father told her that she would be the lucky bride on Rachel's wedding night, why didn't she protest on behalf of her sister? Was this the moment she had always dreamed of? That Rachel the "beauty," Rachel the "favorite," for the first time in her life would not get what she wanted? While she, Leah, the one who everyone overlooked, would finally come out on top? Somewhere in the back of her mind, Leah must have thought she could make it work. Much to her chagrin, she found out that try as she might to win Jacob's affections (even going as far as trying love potions), nothing would work.

"During wheat harvest, Reuben went out into the fields and found some mandrake plants, which he brought to his mother Leah. Rachel said to Leah, 'Please give me some of your son's mandrakes.' But she said to her, 'Wasn't it enough that you took away my husband? Will you take my son's mandrakes too?'" (Genesis 30:14,15 NIV).

Can you imagine Rachel's reaction to Leah's statement? I always get this picture in my mind of Rachel, her hand on her hip, taking a step back and asking in an incredulous tone, "*Your* husband? I hate to be the one to break the news, but might I remind you he was in love with *me*, not you." Somewhere along the way the "other woman" slips comfortably into the deception that she is entitled to this man. "This is the way of an adulteress: She eats and wipes her mouth and says, 'I've done nothing wrong'" (Proverbs 30:20 NIV).

Meanwhile, the "other woman" thinks that the wife is full of shortcomings above which only she rises. This attitude is usually assisted by the unfaithful husband, who has a list of complaints about his spouse that he uses to play on the "other woman's" sympathy and evoke feelings of protectiveness, such as, "She doesn't understand me." And let's not forget the classic line, "I'm getting a divorce." But the catch-22 is that if the "other woman" manages to get her man, she spends the rest of her days living in insecurity. Trust is shattered. How can she be sure this same man who cheated *with* her won't cheat *on* her? Though she feels justified in laying claim to her man, she battles with the fear that she must forever stay one step ahead of him in order to keep his affections. He, in turn, feels the pressure, and she is no longer the pleasant escape she once was. She has now become a worse situation than the one from which he walked away. Or a situation too close for comfort.

If you are in this situation and you are the "other woman," don't fall for the devil's deception that you've finally found your soul mate and he married the wrong person. It might be true that he married the wrong person, but now he is married and God expects him to honor that covenant. You are in God's way if you are standing between that man and his wife. "No one can serve two masters. Either he will hate the one and love the other, or he will be devoted to the one and despise the other" (Matthew 6:24 NIV).

As long as you are in the picture, he will always find something else to dislike in his wife. This is not God's will for your life, no matter how right it feels to you right now. It will never be His will for you to destroy someone else's family in order to have your own. God wants to give you your own husband, free from suspicion and covert activity. To settle for less than God's ideal for you is to grasp at a mirage, only to find there is no water in the pool. The fulfillment you long for in love will never be found in the arms of another woman's husband, even if you finally secure him to be your own.

> "'Stolen water is sweet; food eaten in secret is delicious!' But little do they know that the dead are there, that her guests are in the depths of the grave" (Proverbs 9:17,18 NIV).

God cannot and will not bless a mess. Therefore, anything that starts off wrong generally never gets set aright.

> "What causes fights and quarrels among you? Don't they come from your desires that battle within you? You want something but don't get it. You kill and covet, but you cannot have what you want. You

quarrel and fight. You do not have, because you do not ask God. When you ask, you do not receive, because you ask with wrong motives, that you may spend what you get on your pleasures" (James 4:1-3 NIV).

Covetousness, envy, and jealousy will always cause us to lose. In the first chapter of 1 Samuel, it says that two women, Peninnah and Hannah, were married to the same man. Peninnah had children. Hannah had none. She had been barren for quite some time, but she minded her own business. Still, Peninnah took it upon herself to irritate and provoke Hannah and rub it in her face that she had no children. But as they say, every dog has its day. Hannah got on her face before God, and she was blessed with a beautiful son whom she dedicated to the Lord, as I mentioned in an earlier chapter. This son went on to be a very famous, very important person in Israel, while there is no further mention of Peninnah's children. God honors a heart that is in the right place. It is never wise to celebrate the seeming misfortunes or shortcomings of others.

"But if you harbor bitter envy and selfish ambition in your hearts, do not boast about it or deny the truth. Such 'wisdom' does not come down from heaven but is earthly, unspiritual, of the devil. For where you have envy and selfish ambition, there you find disorder and every evil practice" (James 3:14-16 NIV).

Envy causes the heart to harden. Once hardened, it is filled with murderous thoughts. These thoughts are justified in the hearts of those who covet. It causes them to seek the emotional or physical harm of anyone who stands between them and what they want. It is the bridge to sins that they once swore they would never commit, things that they said they would never do or say, things that sound foreign to their own ears even as their lips spout insults and criticisms that should never be uttered. Lips curl in disdain. Eyes flash with resentment. Bodies tense from subdued fury. These things don't just occur in adulterous affairs. They can arise simply over the attention of a man or the imagined influence once held in his life that now seems threatened by the entry of someone new in his world.

Sister, Sister

Miriam was just too upset. Her brother Moses had gone and married an Ethiopian woman! This was more than she could stand. She had never really had to deal with Zipporah, his first wife from Midian, but this new wife! She was an unwelcome influence who had her brother's ear. And besides, she was not one of them—she was black, she was different, she was an outsider.

It seems that Miriam had lost her standing, at least in her mind, and wanted it back badly. So badly that she began to speak against her own brother and stir up her other brother, Aaron, to be in agreement with her against Moses. They decided that Moses was getting too big for his britches. Miriam was the one who had always been there for Moses. She had watched him sailing down the Nile in a basket as an infant. It was she who was the conduit between Pharaoh's daughter and Moses' mother so that he could be nursed by the one who had given him birth. It was she who stood by his side when he returned from exile to lead the people of Israel out of Egypt. She had always been there, and now this!

Obviously, Miriam felt she had lost her place of influence in Moses' life ever since he had brought his Nubian princess home. Ignoring the fact that she was unwilling to give up the reins to another, Miriam instead began to resent the newcomer. She had always been the one to give input to Moses, and now she did not have the same type of access. So why should she listen to him? After all, she could hear God for herself. So she talked against Moses. Talked against his wife. Until God got irritated. It was clear that God judged her in two areas based on how He addressed her. Though He spoke to both her and Aaron, it was Miriam who got punished because she had started all the confusion. First, God was quick to remind her that though He spoke to them also, His relationship with Moses was different and must be respected. Second, He allowed what was inside of her to be manifested on the outside of her. Envy and strife is ugly, disgusting, and leprous. He struck her with leprosy for seven days. Ironically, God allowed Miriam to get a taste of her own medicine. She would now see how it felt to be judged and ostracized on the basis of her skin. And for seven days she got to think about how it felt to be judged for something you could do nothing about. For seven days she was banned outside of the camp because her condition was unclean. Covetousness and jealousy is nasty and unattractive. It is a turnoff that no man likes to behold. No matter what we think of our other sisters, it behooves us all to watch not only what goes into our mouths, but also what comes out of them.

> "Jesus called the crowd to him and said, 'Listen and understand. What goes into a man's mouth does not make him "unclean," but what comes out of his

mouth, that is what makes him "unclean""
(Matthew 15:10,11 NIV).

Remember Martha and Mary? Two sisters with two very different temperaments. Martha was a go-getter, always having to be busy doing something. Mary was more the live-

---

We must remember once again that we are the manifested heart of God. Men learn from women how to treat women. Our relationships with one another set the standard of treatment for men to follow.

---

in-the-moment type of person. And Martha wasn't having it. All she knew was that while she was killing herself in the kitchen, Mary was just ducking work, sitting at the feet of Jesus. When Martha brought this to Jesus' attention, He was quick to rebuke her and point out that Mary had chosen to do the better thing. Jesus appreciated Martha's service, but what was more important to Him was Mary taking the time for fellowship, to sit at His feet and learn of Him. After all,

His time with them was limited. Any woman can put a meal together, but it takes a special woman to be attuned to her intuitive nature. Mary was spiritually sensitive. It was this same Mary who poured ointment on the feet of Jesus and wiped them with her hair. Mary understood that her first priority was worshiping Jesus, that there would be plenty of time to serve Him later. Jesus was gently telling Martha that there were a few things she could learn from Mary.

This is a special feminine treasure—the ability of women to learn from one another. When women take the time to nourish one another and exchange their gifts, the fruit that comes from those lives is rich! When a group of women gathers to pray or to comfort a friend who is going through trial or heartbreak, the atmosphere is charged with power and healing. When women laugh together, cry together, or simply hold one another when there are no more words to say, it is an inexpressible wonder. Men enjoy watching these exchanges between women. Men envy our ability to nurture and console one another in the same way the angels wonder at us rejoicing over salvation. They haven't got a clue. They do not relate like we do, and yet they wish they could. The world men live in is fraught with competition on another level far beyond what we comprehend. It causes them to hide and guard their jewels closely, even when they are in pain. But women, well, we pull everything out for all to behold. We nurse and rehearse it until we've squeezed the last bit of pain out of it, and in that we are liberated to move on.

The instructions are pretty clear on the design of woman-to-man relationships, but perhaps we need some clarification when it comes to woman-to-woman relationships. What are we supposed to be doing? What does God expect of us? We must remember once again that we are the manifested heart of God. Men learn from women how to treat women. Our relationships with one another set the standard of treatment for men to follow.

Our character is judged by how much integrity we have toward one another. If we assist men in being unfaithful by entering into adulterous relationships with them, they will feel that their behavior is acceptable. If every woman in this country declared a moratorium on infidelity and refused to be involved with men who were married or in committed relationships, men would straighten up and apply themselves to building sound homes and good marriages because they would have no other option. If women refused to talk about one another, sabotage one another, and destroy one another with our looks, words, and attitudes, you would see men lining up, treating us as they should. They merely reflect what they see.

Tearing down someone else does not build us up in the sight of one another. It simply reveals how low we would go to gain attention ourselves. And that is not a pretty picture. But as women begin to rise up and cover one another with love and respect, a different day will dawn between men and women. I dare to say that their respect meters for us would also rise to a whole new level. Remember, if you don't respect yourself and your sisters around you, it is guaranteed that you will attract a disrespectful man.

> "Love must be sincere. Hate what is evil; cling to what is good. Be devoted to one another in [sisterly] love. Honor one another above yourselves....Live in harmony with one another" (Romans 12:9,10,16 NIV).

"If you have any encouragement from being united with Christ, if any comfort from his love, if any fellowship with the Spirit, if any tenderness and compassion, then make my joy complete by being like-minded, having the same love, being one in spirit and purpose. Do nothing out of selfish ambition or vain conceit, but in humility consider others better than yourselves. Each of you should look not only to your own interests, but also to the interests of others. Your attitude should be the same as that of Christ Jesus" (Philippians 2:1-5 NIV).

"If anyone says, 'I love God,' yet hates [her sister], [she] is a liar. For anyone who does not love [her sister], whom [she] has seen, cannot love God, whom [she] has not seen. And he has given us this command: Whoever loves God must also love [her sister]" (1 John 4:20,21 NIV).

"Therefore encourage one another and build each other up....Live in peace with each other" (1 Thessalonians 5:11,13 NIV).

I think that just about sums it up, wouldn't you say? Now some will try to get literal here and say, "Well, I don't hate her, I just don't like her." But if you don't like her, there is no way you could be thinking good thoughts or praying blessings for her. I'm talking about being free enough to celebrate another woman's triumphs and weep for her tragedies. That is the kind of sister love God wants us to have for one another. It is that kind of love that serves men notice, before they even consider mistreating a woman, that this sort of behavior will not be tolerated. He will have to answer to a group of supportive sisters.

"They don't speak to me," my lunch partner told me in hushed tones as a group of young ladies strolled past us in the restaurant. "What do you mean?" I asked, not quite getting it. Perhaps I am a bit naïve, but I'm actually one of those Christians who believes that we should just love everybody. Especially if we've just come from church! The glow of the anointing should hang around for at least an hour or so before we go back to being carnal. Just joking. But really, I was totally confused here. We had just left church and here were these women snubbing my friend. For what reason? Jealousy? She was a pretty girl, but they were also attractive. So I decided to find out. Pretending ignorance, I pulled them into our conversation, which I could see went against their natural instincts. But by the time lunch was over, they were all complimenting one another, quite surprised to find that they all had things in common and actually really liked one another. They had just never taken the time to find this out. My gracious young friend, who these other women had decided was a snob based on her attractive looks, actually had some tidbits to share with them that were quite helpful. In the end they appreciated the exchange.

How much is missed when we refuse to be open to those around us, based on presumptuous assessments of one another. Our time and energy could be put to much better use. We should be busy helping one another prepare to receive blessings, helping one another look the best we can look and exchanging sound advice and encouragement. When the Shulamite woman enlisted the help of her friends to find out where her man had gone, the women asked her, "How is your beloved better than others, most beautiful of women? How is your beloved better than others, that you charge us so?" (Song of Songs 5:9 NIV). In other words, how does he qualify for your affections? What makes him worth the trouble? Well, Shulamite began to run down a list of his qualities, from his wavy hair to the sweetness of his mouth, and the women all rose up and said, "Where has your lover gone, most beautiful of women? Which way did your lover turn, that we may look for him with you?" (Song of Songs 6:1 NIV). They were willing to help her! They celebrated her beauty and set a standard for their sister. This man had to deserve her, he had to match her beauty. With all that in place, they were ready and willing to celebrate their union and assist in any way they could to bring these two together.

We will reap what we sow. What you make happen for others, God will make happen for you. As we purpose to build up another sister to help her step into the fullness of all that awaits her, we will reap our own reward. After all, you never know who is watching. When Ruth decided to leave Moab and follow Naomi back to Israel, she left behind all hopes of ever remarrying. She was sold out to the care of her mother-in-law. While she was busy about the business of doing what was necessary for their survival, people began taking note of her care of Naomi. They began to talk amongst themselves. They considered Ruth to be a pretty special woman. What wonderful character she must have had to leave her own homeland and embrace such a difficult existence! This talk got all the way back to a man named Boaz, who owned a field where Ruth just happened to be gleaning wheat one day. He noticed her physically, but he noted her based on her sterling reputation which had gone before her. The rest is history. Ruth ended up with a wealthy husband and became the great-grandmother of David, king of Israel, thereby entering into the lineage of Jesus Christ. It is important to note that all of this came about as Ruth followed the wise advice of Naomi.

In a society that seldom sees the value in our senior citizens, I must repeat what I heard as a child: "They didn't get old by being a fool." Older people have valuable lessons for us to learn. They have tried, failed, and succeeded at going where we still want to go. When you are going on a trip, doesn't it make sense to consult with someone who has already been there? It saves you time and trouble. You can go and enjoy the journey, armed with the knowledge of what—and what not—to see and do. Such is life. Mentoring is extremely important. Having an older woman speak into your life is one of the greatest gifts you can acquire. And then it is your duty to pass that information on to someone younger than yourself. For two years I was the guardian of my two nieces from Africa while they attended school in this country. It was a joy for me to teach them the ways of women—grooming, manners, things from God's Word on how to be young women who would someday be treasured by a man. I taught them how to love and celebrate one another, and to celebrate themselves and the incredible gift of womanhood they had been given. They blossomed and others around them noticed the difference, and that was my reward. It is crucially important for women to affirm one another. We hold the key to one another's wholeness.

> "The aged women likewise, that they be in behaviour as becometh holiness, not false accusers, not given to much wine, teachers of good things; that they may teach the young women to be sober, to love their husbands, to love their children, to be discreet, chaste, keepers at home, good, obedient to

their own husbands, that the word of God be not blasphemed" (Titus 2:3-5 KJV).

From both of my fathers I have learned what standard to set for the man in my life. From my mother I have learned how to be a woman. Her advice has always been sound, whether I liked it or not. Her counsel has always proven to be correct. I wouldn't trade her for the world. She is my mother and my friend, as all of the women in my family have proven to be. Over the years I have rejoiced in rich friendships with women. We have fussed, encouraged, rebuked, and celebrated one another and come out the better for it. As a single woman, I have had my good days and my bad days. But my good days outweigh my bad days because of the support and encouragement of my sisters, women walking together in unity, determined to see God's best coming to fruition in my life. This is my prayer for all women, that they will find the beauty in one another and reconcile their differences. Then and only then will we be able to erase the misconceptions of men and win them by our blameless example.

> "Now that you have purified yourselves by obeying the truth so that you have sincere love for your [sisters], love one another deeply from the heart" (1 Peter 1:22 NIV).

> "How good and pleasant it is when [sisters] live together in unity" (Psalm 133:1 NIV).

This is where the healing between the sexes begins! It begins with us.

> "As it is, there are many parts, but one body. The eye cannot say to the hand, 'I don't need you!' And

the head cannot say to the feet, 'I don't need you!'...But God has combined the members of the body and has given greater honor to the parts that lacked it, so that there should be no division in the body, but that its parts should have equal concern for each other. If one part suffers, every part suffers with it; if one part is honored, every part rejoices with it" (1 Corinthians 12:20,21,24-26 NIV).

Dear Heavenly Father, I ask Your forgiveness for my wrongful attitudes toward my sisters. But even more so for not trusting You. For feeling that I had to make my own way. Secure my own destiny. I have fought and striven with my sisters in the process. I have allowed my own insecurities to affect my heart against those who really had no control over what You have designed for my life. Help me to rest in You, understanding that every good and perfect gift for my life comes from Your hands and cannot be hindered by the arm of flesh. Help me to celebrate the blessings of my sisters, knowing You are not a respecter of persons. What You do for one, You will also do for me. I will to forgive those who have hurt me. I ask that You will mend the breach between myself and _____ . That You will help me to reconcile my heart to release the offenses that have stopped the flow of love in my life. Cleanse me and prepare my heart to love and be loved, to encourage and be encouraged, to provoke others to good works and the fullness of who You have called them to be as women, to promote and edify, even as You shape and mold me into Your image. In Jesus' name. Amen.

SIX

How to Build Your House

She opened the windows
allowing the Son to fill the room
filling his world with light
this man to which she said "I do"
with promises of to have and to hold
for richer
or poorer
in sickness
and in health
till death do us part
amen
took in his surroundings
as she
the reflection of love in his eyes
parted curtains of contentment
allowing a breeze of inspiration
to cool his brow...
an oasis
yes, that's what this home was
an oasis
a place of refreshment
and healing
from all the outside world inflicted
as she greeted him
with tender embraces
and adoration
serving him encouragement
and solace
piping hot and delicious
followed with a thick coating of
soothing

"you-can-make-it
because-I'm-here-for-you" sauce
her hand traced creative patterns on his shoulders
chasing away worry and tension
while the scent of her
caused him to have pleasant amnesia
about the cares of the day
home was not only
where his heart was
it was where his treasure abode
growing more precious as the
years went by
sparkling in her eyes
as she viewed her handiwork
and the delight he took in it...
this miniature world
that belonged to them alone...
yes, he was home...

$\mathcal{R}$ebekah saw the lone man standing in the distance, studying her intently. Clearly he was not from these parts. He had the look of a well-worn traveler and her heart softened as she sensed his weariness. How could she refuse when he asked for a drink? There was a kindness in his face that appealed to her sense of giving. Surely his camels needed watering as well. It was the least she could do. She would want someone to do the same for her brothers if they had traveled so far. This she did with no thought of reward, only of the satisfaction she experienced from performing an act of kindness. So pleasant was her surprise when she was presented with the substantial gift of gold jewelry. And, pleasure upon pleasure, this man was the servant of relatives in a far-away land! As she ran to call her father and brothers, she marveled on how this had all come about. An ordinary day was suddenly filled with excitement in a matter of moments. How many times had she gone to draw water at the well, day after day, and returned home with no special occurrences along the way?

But today was like no other day. No, this was entirely different. The servant was asking if she would give her hand in marriage to his master! Truly, this was the Lord's doing. She couldn't believe it, yet she heard herself agreeing to go with him to live the rest of her days with a man she had never seen. Yet she felt such peace. Throughout the journey she rehearsed a hundred times her greeting to this mystery man. She plied the servant with questions. What was her husband like? Was he kind? Obviously he was successful, but was he handsome, too? However, men never seemed to be able to gauge if other men were attractive, so that she would have to see for herself. Would he be romantic and expressive? Would he be the man she'd always dreamed of marrying? So many pieces of a puzzle! She could not yet see how they fit together in any kind of significant order. Though the journey seemed to take forever, still it ended too soon when she finally stood before him, searching for the words she had rehearsed over and over in her mind.

This was it. This was no fantasy. He was real. Handsome and kind and real. Their marriage was real and immediate. As he took her into his mother's tent, she breathed a prayer that she, too, would be all that he had dreamed of. So she became his wife, and he loved her, and was comforted after his mother's death.

What Wives Are Made Of

"What do I have to offer?" my girlfriend was asking me. "I'm still at home with my parents with nothing to show for myself. What do I have to offer a man?" As I come from a cross-cultural background of African and West Indian descent, this was a nonsensical question to me. What did she

mean, what did she have to offer to a man? She was a wonderful woman with extraordinary gifts that, no doubt, would
make some man deliriously happy when he found her. I
thought of myself and how many times *my* home had been a
source of intimidation to men who had started pursuing me.
Mind you, I am not saying that we should put our lives on
hold until Mr. Wonderful shows up so that he can feel that
he is truly rescuing us from an unfortunate fate. At the age
of forty, this would not be a good testimony. I bring this up
only to point out that many men feel they have nothing to
offer most women because the women have gotten it all for
themselves. And we confirm this by wearing a self-sufficient
attitude, leaving no room for the man to feel as if he can add
anything else to our world. We must be careful of this. But
the greater point I am trying to make is that everything a
woman has to offer to a man is actually *within* her. It is not
in the accumulation of outer trappings. Many women have
all the externals together but still don't have a clue about
the needs of a man or know how to please him.

I took it upon myself to inform my friend that this whole
phenomenon of people living independently before marriage
is really an American concept. In other countries—Euro-
pean, Asian, and Third World—men and women live at
home with their parents until they have married. Sometimes,
depending on the financial status of a family and the dimen-
sions of the family estate, the couple might remain in the
family home *after* they are married. This is not really a foreign
concept; it is a biblical one. Men and women remained with
their parents until they were prepared to leave. The man
worked until he had a home prepared for his bride, and then
she went to live with her husband. She was only released to

that man after he had made provision for her care and security. Now, isn't that a fine concept?

Actually, it is a rather smart one. Economically, countries where this is practiced have more people who are financially sound. Their homes are usually paid for and have been in the family for years so no one has to scrape up rent. They contribute to the upkeep of everything else amongst themselves and bank the main part of their earnings or invest it in more property. Emotionally, daughters are more secure because men with bad intentions are less likely to brave the protective observance of a father. Also, familial community living keeps everyone from growing selfish. The adjustment to marriage is helped because people have never lived in an isolated environment and grown attached to having their "own space" and individual way of doing things.

This goes all the way back to Jesus, the ultimate bridegroom, who said, "I am going there to prepare a place for you. And if I go and prepare a place for you, I will come back and take you to be with me that you also may be where I am" (John 14:2,3 NIV). And that's not all! His Father is preparing the ultimate wedding feast for us. Now, what is expected of the bride? The bride is expected to show up wearing pure garments, ready to worship. That's it. We'll cover worship in a later chapter, but for now you've got to take note that all the bridegroom really wants or expects is a woman who has kept herself for him and him alone and the understanding of what it takes to make him feel good. That's what worship and praise does for anyone. Worship and praise extends beyond just vocal utterance; it extends to your care of someone, what you do to make his world a pleasurable place to be.

I must interject something here because I receive many, many letters on this subject, and I don't want anyone falling into condemnation on the purity issue. Everyone in the body of Christ, dare I say most, have not been saved all of their lives. And many others, in and out of the church, are struggling to maintain control over their flesh. Some have been married before, widowed, or divorced. Therefore, the percentage of actual "virgins" per capita is a minority. For those of you who are tempted to feel you are not worthy wife material because of your past, let us set the record straight once and for all. This is why Jesus died. He died for all sin. When He said *all* sin, He meant *all* sin. Now, I know some of you think that your particular sins are special, but trust me, they fall under the category of *all* sin. There is no sin stain so deep that God can't get it out.

> "'Come now, let us reason together,' says the LORD. 'Though your sins are like scarlet, they shall be as white as snow; though they are red as crimson, they shall be like wool'" (Isaiah 1:18 NIV).

> "You will again have compassion on us; you will...hurl all our iniquities into the depths of the sea" (Micah 7:19 NIV).

> "For I will forgive their wickedness and will remember their sins no more" (Jeremiah 31:34 NIV).

> "Forget the former things; do not dwell on the past. See, I am doing a new thing! Now it springs up; do you not perceive it?" (Isaiah 43:18,19 NIV).

> "Not that I have already obtained all this, or have already been made perfect, but I press on to take hold of that for which Christ Jesus took hold of me. Brothers, I do not consider myself yet to have taken hold of it. But one thing I do: *Forgetting what is behind*

and straining toward what is ahead, I press on toward the goal to win the prize for which God has called me heavenward in Christ Jesus" (Philippians 3:12-14 NIV, emphasis added).

I hope this has been enough to convince you that sitting around nursing and rehearsing your past is not the way to go. That is false condemnation, and Satan loves to use it to paralyze you from moving forward. Everyone has a past, God bless the few who don't, and that's why we all need Jesus. Men included. They come bringing their own baggage. If you have confessed your sins to God, you don't need to continually discuss them with anyone else. Unless something in your past now affects your health or would become an issue in your new marriage, I suggest you leave your experiences under the blood and keep them between yourself and Jesus. There is a difference between blatantly confessing and having a testimony. To give illicit details about every little thing you've ever done is self-defeating. It stirs up things in your spirit that are better left dormant. Satan uses this area very subtly. It becomes an area of pride. As if our stepping into a new life were some Olympian triumph on our part: "See how good I am now? Well, you would never believe how bad I was before! Look at triumphant me!" Don't rejoice in that, rather rejoice in the fact that you've been redeemed by a loving Savior who thought you a precious jewel, worthy to die for. And if He thought you were worthy to die for, then believe me, any man in his right mind will think you worthy to marry, regardless of your past mistakes. Why? Because they are looking at the new you, the redeemed you. The you that has been washed clean in the blood of the Lamb. Because of Jesus, as you allow Him to keep your body, you can consider yourself a virgin again. All a good man is looking for is a woman of godly principle who walks in purity and knows how to worship. And that's who you are now!

Nothing affects a man as deeply as an encounter with a woman who has womanly qualities.

One of my friends was addressing a group of women at a conference and said, "A man wants three things—to be well-fed, well-loved in the sexual sense, and well-appreciated." One woman rose up and irately asked, "And what do I get out of it?" Quite surprised the woman even had to ask, my friend replied, "Why, you'll be well-loved, well-kept, and well-satisfied!" I've listened to my male friends. They love feminine women. Nothing affects a man as deeply as an encounter with a woman who has womanly qualities. They literally purr when they recall their interaction with her.

Rebekah was a virgin and she went to meet Isaac with nothing except her clothing and a maidservant. But she went packing a whole lot more inside. Because she grew up surrounded by brothers, she had learned the ways of men. We know from her first encounter with her prospective husband's servant that she understood how to serve a man. She understood the value of his possessions and respected them as things to be cared for as well. She conducted herself like a lady, yielded to the decision of her father and brothers, took a giant leap of faith, and got the bonus prize. The Bible says that Isaac loved her and was comforted by her. Rebekah was a woman who had warmth. She was attractive and loving. She was a good cook—this we know from later on when she cooks up a delicious stew in order to help her son Jacob get the blessing. She knew how to make a house a home. Whether you have a man or not, you should do these things. Begin to practice on the men who are already in your world. If you are single, your brothers, cousins, and friends can help you to prepare for being a good mate and homemaker. So, man or no man, do it for yourself and your own sense of completion. Do it for your loved ones and your friends. Do it as a testimony to the grace within you.

There is something to be said for waking up in the morning and being pleased that you've made your home the best home it could be, no matter how simple or elaborate it is. This is important because your home reflects who you are. When people leave your home, they should leave with a sense of knowing something about you they didn't know before. When people walk into your apartment or house, their mood should change. The atmosphere of your home should reflect peace and well-being. People should sense the presence of God in your home. It should be an oasis for thirsty, weary souls.

But your home is more than just your physical house; it is your household. It is the hearts of those who surround you. The heart is where we all really live. Therefore, the flavor your spirit brings to the mix extends beyond the idea of the walls you live within. It is the way everyone under your roof is affected by your presence. You get to set the stage for how everyone feels—children, mate, friends, yourself. I recall visiting some friends in New York awhile back. The woman of the house worked unusual hours, so she was out most of the day. When she arrived home, the whole atmosphere changed. It was as if the sun had come out in the middle of the evening. Suddenly the house came alive. Everyone was happy and excited. The air was charged with love and the anticipation of a wonderful time before everyone retired for the night. All of this because of one woman who possessed a sweet spirit, a gentle way, and a contagious laugh.

> "The wise woman builds her house, but with her own hands the foolish one tears hers down" (Proverbs 14:1 NIV).

Everything revolves around the woman of the house. I love the title of a delightful book, *When Mama Ain't Happy, Ain't Nobody Happy* (Lindsey O'Conner, Harvest House). And that's the truth. Just take a look at how a woman affects a house.

> "Better to live on the corner of the roof than share a house with a quarrelsome wife" (Proverbs 21:9 NIV).

"Better to live in a desert than with a quarrelsome and ill-tempered wife" (Proverbs 21:19 NIV).

"A quarrelsome wife is like a constant dripping on a rainy day" (Proverbs 27:15 NIV).

"A foolish woman is clamorous, she is simple, and knows nothing" (Proverbs 9:13 NKJV).

"Like a gold ring in a pig's snout is a beautiful woman who shows no discretion" (Proverbs 11:22 NIV).

"For three things the earth is perturbed, yes for…a hateful woman when she is married" (Proverbs 30:21,23 NKJV).

"A wife of noble character is her husband's crown, but a disgraceful wife is like decay in his bones" (Proverbs 12:4 NIV).

That about sums it up. A woman can make life so miserable for a man that he would rather abide in the desert. Her attitude can eat up a man and completely destroy him. She can choose to use the power she has to make him or break him. She is his protection. The man is called to walk in front of the woman to ward off opposition and danger, but the woman has been created to surround that man and protect his heart. I'm still speaking to the single women here, as well. Every man who crosses your path should feel better when he is in your presence. You have a wonderful opportunity to perfect your gifts while you are single. Learn how to build your house now.

What is a house? What is its function exactly? Well, a house wards off the elements. It covers you in times of rain, storms, heat, cold, snow, anything that could affect your health. It keeps you warm in the winter and cool in the summer. It harbors all of your possessions and keeps them safe. It gives you safe boundaries and consistency; you return to the same place every day. It provides access to others, as people know where to come to find you. It offers you a place to feed, rest, and even to cleanse yourself.

As a wife, or a godly woman, the man in your life should feel that his heart, his secrets, and his emotions are safe with you. You should be the one to contribute to regulating his emotions and decisions, cooling him down when he's hot under the collar, and fanning the flame to stir up his passion for God, his ambitions, and his home. You should be his haven of consistency, the one who is always there, the one he can always count on. He knows what to expect from you because your character is so sound. He should not come home every day to find a different woman who he can't figure out living in his house. He should have access to your heart, your softness, your reassurances, and your counsel all the time, and vice versa. You should be his oasis. He should be refreshed in your presence. And because of your good example, he wants to be the best he can be for you. He will put away anything that could sully him in your eyes. Nothing on the face of the earth affects a man like the softness of a woman. Of all the things that he may acquire in his lifetime, nothing can bring him more joy or pain than to be welcomed or spurned by the woman he longs after.

> "You have stolen my heart, my sister, my bride; you have stolen my heart with one glance of your eyes.... How delightful is your love, my sister, my bride! How much more pleasing is your love than wine, and the fragrance of your perfume than any spice! Your lips

drop sweetness as the honeycomb, my bride; milk
and honey are under your tongue.... You are a garden
locked up, my sister, my bride; you are a spring
enclosed, a sealed fountain.... You are a garden fountain, a well of flowing water streaming down from
Lebanon" (Song of Songs 4:9-12,15 NIV).

When a man is in love, he is in love. "Can't keep his mind
on nothin' else," as the song goes. Solomon was deeply in
love with the Shulamite woman. Why? The girl knew how
to build a house. One glance into her eyes—eyes filled with
trust and adoration—leveled him. Loving her was a pleasure.
She looked good, smelled good, and was a delight to be
around. Her love was intoxicating. And she always had
something sweet to say. The girl had a rap that left him
speechless. She walked in purity and she was discreet. Therefore, she had his trust. She was downright refreshing. She
was a sanctuary, a beautiful garden in which he loved to get
lost. This was where he found his peace.

Construction 101

Because most men will agree that a house is not a home
until the feminine touch has been applied, I think we now
need to make sure we're all equipped with the right tools.
How do we build a good, solid house in which a man can
feel at home? Well, let's begin with a sound foundation of
trust.

Solomon spoke of the Shulamite being a sealed fountain,
meaning that she had kept her love for him. She had not
slept with other men. She had self-control. Her "fountain"
was for her husband only. Because she had exercised restraint
before meeting him and kept it until their wedding day, he

could trust her when he was away from her. If he could trust her to keep her own vessel, he could then trust her to keep the things pertaining to him, as well. Men don't trust many people in their outside world. Therefore, a man needs to know he can trust his woman. Ask any man his pet peeve, and he'll tell you that he hates it when the woman in his life discusses his business with her friends—his business being your relationship. Discretion is important to a man. What you choose to shout abroad can lead to his undoing. The man in your life needs to know he can hide his heart, his dreams, and his secrets with you. He needs to know that he can trust you to handle the situations that arise between the two of you discreetly, free of panic, without sounding every alarm.

In 1 Samuel, chapter 25, we find a woman who had this down to a science. Perhaps because Abigail's husband, Nabal, was a fool, and that was not a fact she wished to broadcast, she learned to handle his mistakes quietly and without drawing attention to him. When King David was camping out on Nabal's territory, he and his troops ran out of food. So he sent word to Nabal asking for provisions. Because his troops had been protecting Nabal's flocks and crops, David thought this was a fair exchange. But Nabal foolishly chose to insult David and his men. David became very angry and vowed to destroy Nabal and his household. One of Nabal's servants then went to Abigail to inform her about what was happening. Summing up what had happened, he said something very interesting: "Now think it over and see what you can do, because disaster is hanging over our master and his whole household. He is such a wicked man that no one can talk to him" (1 Samuel 25:17 NIV). Why did the servant feel that he could go to Abigail? Because she was "a woman of good understanding, and of a beautiful countenance" (1 Samuel 25:3 KJV). She had sense, and she was approachable, kind, and discerning! She didn't fuss at her husband; she quietly took action. She gathered the provisions needed, then set off to appease David.

And though David was not a member of her household, she did a little housekeeping with him, too. She politely reminded him that he had a call on his life much greater than the attention this situation was getting. He should preserve his wrath for more important battles, staying focused on God's plan for his life and not adding needless bloodshed to his credit. She believed in his destiny, so much so that she asked him to remember her when the Lord brought him into success. David was quick to tell her that if it hadn't been for her, every male belonging to Nabal would have been dead by daybreak. Because of her, his wrath was assuaged. "A gracious woman retaineth honour" (Proverbs 11:16 KJV).

So Abigail went home to find her husband having a party. Did she tap him on the shoulder and proceed to tell him a thing or two right there and then? No, she held her peace until morning, and then she respectfully related everything that had happened. The moment the story was told, something happened to Nabal. He had a stroke, fell into a coma, or had a heart attack. Who can say? But his end came ten days later when the Lord struck him and he died. When David heard of Nabal's death, he sent for Abigail to become his wife. He knew a good thing when he saw one. This brings me back to my point about single women absorbing this information. I'll repeat what I said earlier: You never know who is watching you. Abigail was not looking at David as husband material. She was merely protecting her house. Little did she know that she was planting seeds for her future.

And what a harvest it was! She became a wife to the king of Israel.

Now that we have our foundation in place, let's deal with the frame. Prudence will keep a house firm no matter what is going on within its walls. Prudence is a precious commodity.

> "Houses and wealth are inherited from parents, but a prudent wife is from the LORD" (Proverbs 19:14 NIV).

> "A [woman] who lacks judgment derides [her] neighbor, but a [woman] of understanding holds [her] tongue" (Proverbs 11:12 NIV).

> "A prudent [woman] keeps [her] knowledge to [herself], but the heart of fools blurts out folly" (Proverbs 12:23 NIV).

> "Every prudent [woman] acts out of knowledge, but a fool exposes [her] folly" (Proverbs 13:16 NIV).

> "The wise in heart are called prudent, understanding, and knowing, and winsome speech increases learning [in both speaker and listener]. Understanding is a wellspring of life to those who have it, but to give instruction to fools is folly. The mind of the wise instructs [her] mouth, and adds learning and persuasiveness to [her] lips. Pleasant words are as a honeycomb, sweet to the mind and healing to the body" (Proverbs 16:21-24 AMP).

Now you know why Abigail didn't waste her time saying anything to Nabal. She knew that it would be useless. She chose her battles and left the rest to the Lord. And the Lord showed up in a major way on her behalf. Take a lesson from Abigail. Why break the spirit of a man to make a point? Just take care of your house. If he is worth salvaging, God will deal with him. If he's not, God will take him out. The end, by God. Prudence sees the big picture and acts accordingly. It doesn't major in the minors or minor in the majors. It assesses a situation and takes decisive action, minus all of the unnecessary mess. That is why prudence and wisdom walk hand in hand. If prudence is the frame of the house, then wisdom is the roof. It keeps a lid on all that transpires within its walls. "I, wisdom, dwell together with prudence; I possess knowledge and discretion" (Proverbs 8:12 NIV).

Another translation says that wisdom dwells with prudence and finds out knowledge of witty inventions. Wisdom makes creative use of its knowledge. Every feminine woman knows that there are ways to get things done without wreaking havoc. Back in the days when King David was suffering from the rebellion of his son Absalom, another man named Sheba rose up and caused the children of Israel to rebel against David after he returned home. When David was resettled in the palace, his army went after Sheba. They found him hiding in a city called Abel Beth Maacah, so they built a siege ramp up to the city and began battering the wall of the city to bring it down. The story goes that "a wise woman" called over the wall and asked Joab, who was leading the siege, what he wanted. When he informed her that he was there to take Sheba, she told him, "We are the peaceful and faithful in Israel. You are trying to destroy a city that is a mother in Israel. Why do you want to swallow up the LORD's inheritance?" (2 Samuel 20:18 NIV). Joab replied that this was not his intention; he simply wanted Sheba. She answered that if that was all he wanted, the head of Sheba would be thrown to him from the wall. Notice that she did not get pulled into a long conversation or let the threatening force enter her gates. She just went about the business of doing what had to be done to reverse the course of events. It does not say that she went after Sheba's head herself; she just found a way to make it happen.

She Who Has an Ear

The woman went to all the people in the city with her "wise advice," and they cut off Sheba's head and threw it over the wall. The army dispersed and went its way, and thus the city was saved from destruction—all because of one wise woman. The woman's name was not disclosed, but her story is recorded because of its importance. She had no high position in the city, but she had a reputation for wisdom, and the leaders obviously listened to her. When the army was battering down the wall, no one had made a move except to cower against the impending doom. This one woman asked the wisest question any woman could ever ask her man: "What do you want?" You see, wisdom is wise because she listens. Listen to the man in your life. Find out what he wants, and then give it to him. It keeps the army from destroying your house, your relationship, your state of well-being, and your heart.

> "Catch for us the foxes, the little foxes that ruin the vineyards, our vineyards that are in bloom" (Song of Songs 2:15 NIV).

It's the little bits and pieces falling through the crevices of everyday life that ruin things. The accumulation of requests ignored. The belittling of another's needs and desires. The small offenses overlooked. The lack of accommodating the other's sensitivities. All of a sudden, what started off as a tiny crack in the wall of love has become a leveled wreck. No one can recall quite when the damage took its toll, but now the repair will be very costly.

These women understood that a great part of their purpose was to keep the men in their world centered on the purposes of God being played out to completion in their lives. Every woman is called to affect every man within her sphere of influence in this fashion.

This woman took the time to find out why the city was being attacked. She went beyond what her eyes could see to get to the root of the problem. When the problem was voiced, she found a solution and solicited help bringing it about. It wasn't about her getting the credit, or even saving her own life. It was about something greater than that. Once again, I hope that you are noticing the common thread in all of this—it was about the purposes of God being protected. Abigail brought it up, and the wise woman also brought it up. Everything, every decision made, must be made in the light of God's purposes for our lives and the lives of others. These women understood that a great part of their purpose was to keep the men in their world centered on the purposes of God being played out to completion in their lives. Every woman is called to affect every man within her sphere of influence in this fashion.

Joab was not the wise woman's husband, but nevertheless, he was a man messing with the purposes of God and messing with the destiny of a nation. It took a woman to bring it to his attention. The realization of this brought everything to a screaming halt, and an alternative to the destruction was found. "The fear of the LORD is the beginning of wisdom" (Proverbs 9:10 NIV).

It is God's purposes which supply the mortar that keeps the whole house standing. It is our relationship with Him that furnishes us with true wisdom. Through the guidance of His Holy Spirit instructing us, "This is the way, walk ye in it" (Isaiah 30:21 KJV), we receive fresh advice daily for every situation in our lives and relationships. This is the "daily bread" we need to ask for. Wisdom trusts God completely and is never presumptuous in leaning to its own understanding.

There is something special about a woman who masters the art of gently leading her man to see reason and to make wise decisions for her house. Art is not about manipulation. It is about possessing an understanding of the subject and the appropriate technique of rendering. No two pictures are the same because the artist is sensitive to the object being captured. An artist is cognizant of the limitations of the medium being used. You can't be heavy-handed with water paint; it would ruin the paper. And canvas must be prepared in order for oil or acrylic paint to dry and age properly once the work is complete.

> "The fear of the LORD teaches a [woman] wisdom, and humility comes before honor" (Proverbs 15:33 NIV).

> "A wise [woman's] heart guides [her] mouth, and [her] lips promote instruction" (Proverbs 16:23 NIV).

> "Her ways [wisdom] are pleasant ways, and all her paths are peace" (Proverbs 3:17 NIV).

> "A gentle answer turns away wrath, but a harsh word stirs up anger" (Proverbs 15:1 NIV).

And so the beauty of art is in its originality and technique. God is the greatest artist of all. No two snowflakes are the same. No two women are the same. No two men are the same. We are each unique, bearing our own set of individual needs and idiosyncrasies. Small wonder Paul said this whole marriage thing was a mystery. Imagine—two people walking as one in spite of it all. That is a divine mystery. That is why wisdom, godly wisdom, is required. "Wisdom has built her house; she has hewn out its seven pillars" (Proverbs 9:1 NIV).

Wisdom keeps the house in order and covers it from all forces that threaten to destroy it. What are the seven pillars that make it able to withstand the storms of life and relationships? Prudence, knowledge, discretion, counsel, sound judgment, understanding, and power. God wants every woman to be equipped and fitted with these qualities so she can save her house and the testimonies of the men who surround her.

When the Jews were confronted with a life-and-death situation in the book of Esther, Queen Esther felt that she did
not qualify as a part of the solution. But her uncle, Mordecai,
reminded her that perhaps her position as queen was the only
reason she was where she was. Therefore, she needed to use
her influence to persuade her husband to save her people. In
other words, this is it, girlfriend, if you're a wife, all of your
womanly faculties need to kick in now as never before. This
situation had to be handled carefully, and Esther knew it.
Though she was a godly woman, her husband was not a
believer. He was Persian and worshiped other gods. Knowledge made Esther realize that she could not go sweeping into
his throne room using religion as her argument. She had to
appeal to his senses as a man in order to get what she needed
from him. So after fasting and waiting on the counsel of God
for three days, she took the time to look her best and pay her
husband a visit. When he saw her, he was so pleased that he
offered her half his kingdom. But understanding instructed
Esther not to get caught up in the moment. She needed to
stay focused. Therefore, all she asked for was his presence,
along with Haman's (the man who was a threat to the lives
of her and her people), at a banquet she had prepared for
him.

Can you imagine what that did to his ego? Wisdom knows
that there's a time for everything. After he was well-fed and
feeling adored, the king again offered Esther half of his
kingdom. She responded that her only desire was for him
and Haman to join her again at dinner. Well, he left feeling
pretty special. Esther was exhibiting discretion at its finest.
The threat of death would be enough to make even the
wisest woman panic, but prudence kept watch, waiting for
the opportune time to broach the subject.

When the king returned for a second banquet, again offering her half the kingdom, Esther's sound judgment kicked in. It was time to lay her request before her husband. This was when her power as a woman took control. Still wrapped in femininity, she revealed that her life was in danger and that the lives of her people were at stake. As her distress was revealed, the king rose in a rage. Though the people in trouble were without his house, the life of his wife also affected his own life and house. He demanded to know who was responsible for this. As Esther pointed to the perpetrator, Haman's fate was sealed. He threw himself across Esther's couch, pleading for mercy, but the king decided that he had gotten too close for comfort and ordered him hanged. Haman's house was then given to Esther, who passed it on to Mordecai. A feminine woman will possess the house of her enemies and those who come to cause division and strife. Her house will be established in unity as her husband rises up to be her protector, her cover, and her provider, whether he is godly or not.

Once again, other men were affected besides the husband of Esther. Her influence saved the lives of many men and fulfilled the purposes of God in their lives. And because she chose to build her house with wisdom, her husband yielded to her desires, asking her what else would she like for him to do. Esther made her husband her ally and her hero, and he was pleased to rise to the occasion. And she, in turn, was pleased to dwell beneath his covering. This is the type of house that causes all within its walls to feel secure. A woman submitted to her Lord and King can rest secure in the knowledge that her house is standing on solid ground.

You must take note that wisdom did not just suddenly descend on Esther. She built her personal house first. She had been prepared for "such a time as this" long before she entered the palace of the king. She was already established in her relationship with God. Her feminine skills had been honed in the home of her uncle, as he had taught her the skills needed for making a home as well as the things of God. The eunuchs in the palace added the finishing touches to an already-exquisite vessel as they detailed the finer aspects of the ways of women. Esther was prepared without and within. She was walking in the knowledge that she had acquired before she had been selected to marry the king. Therefore, when crisis struck, she was able to automatically flow in the right manner.

> "Finish your outdoor work and get your fields ready;
> after that, build your house" (Proverbs 24:27 NIV).

Another translation says, "First put all in order out of doors and make everything ready on the land; then establish your house and home" (NEB). In other words, acquire all that you need to know and put it in order and get all that you've learned firmly entrenched in your heart. Then the stage will be set, and you will be ready to build and establish a home. Building takes prep work. You must gather your supplies in the right quantities. And then, with the help of the Lord, the Master Builder, you must become a skillful craftsman. Remember that what you put into your home will affect how it stands. So build your house carefully.

> "Except the LORD builds the house, they labour in
> vain that build it" (Psalm 127:1 KJV).

*Dear Heavenly Father, You are the Potter, and I am the clay.
Build my house. Furnish it with the fruit of the Spirit. Fill it
with the aroma of Your anointing. Decorate me in wisdom and
virtue, that I might be a sanctuary to all who dwell in my presence. Grant me the gift of discernment to truly listen and hear
the needs of others. Teach me the ways of women according to
Your original design. Strengthen me to withstand the tests of
storms and trials. Help me to stand fast when the very founda-
tions of all I believe in and hope for are shaken. As I stand fast
in Your promise to be the Cornerstone that stands firm in my
life, make me an oasis, a quiet place, and a haven for the
hearts of those You send my way. In Jesus' name. Amen.*

SEVEN

The Strength of Vulnerability

She called him Lord
and crowned him with her graciousness
following beside
shielded by his protective arms
she basked in his shadow
all the while being his sun
her rays
bathing him in assurances
of greatness and esteem
whispering wisdoms in his ear
he did not reject
as she dressed him
in success before his peers...
and as her love surrounded his heart
warding off the enemy
he did battle for her
covering that most precious to him
for she was his glory
his treasure
his pearl of great price
she stooped
he stooped even lower
not willing to lose sight of her eyes
eyes that said so much
without saying anything at all
yet they gave him peace
in the middle of a storm
they made him see reason
when his own vision
was clouded with rage
they lit the way

illuminating his path
with sound direction
all the while still calling him Lord
the pressure of gentle hands pushed him onward
toward the fulfillment of his destiny
soothing tired shoulders
stroking away worry
silencing the child
awakening the man within
as only she could
still calling him Lord
she held his world steady in her hands
she filled his empty spaces
she repaired the breaches in his spirit
and made him whole again...
she was his sanctuary
his food
his light
his queen
and still she called him Lord...

*J*ust say you're my sister," Abraham said. Sarah frowned, saying nothing, as she listened to her husband. It was true what he said, but it was also not true. Though she was his half sister, she was also his wife. She could not believe that he wanted her to lie! "I'm not going to stand here and fool myself. I know how beautiful you are. I see the way that men look at you. If the Egyptians know that you're my wife, they'll kill me and take you. But if they think you are my sister, they will treat me well because of you." As Abraham continued, Sarah still said nothing. She would obey even though she disagreed, and she knew that her eyes told him how she felt. This was the same man who had come to her one day, saying that the Lord had told him to leave their home and venture forth to a place He would show them. He had no idea where they were going; he only had this burning knowing that he must follow the call of God. And so Sarah obediently packed up their belongings and followed her husband, praying that God would keep them and honor their obedience.

And now this! Abraham was truly asking a bit much with this new proposition. Hadn't it been enough to ask her to leave the comfort of an established home and longtime friends? Though the consequences of these actions would fall upon his head and not hers, Sarah could not deny that she was dreading seeing how this deception would play out. How her husband could trust God to wander in the land, yet could not trust Him to protect their lives, she did not understand. But rather than question him, she would wait and see what God did. Well, Abraham was right about one thing. The Egyptians did find Sarah beautiful—so beautiful, they raved about her to Pharaoh, and took her into the palace to become Pharaoh's wife! While Abraham was lavished with all sorts of extravagant presents, livestock, and servants, Sarah sat in the palace waiting to see how God was going to get them out of this fine mess. She prayed that God would keep her and protect her from Pharaoh's affections. That was where the line would have to be drawn. And then it happened—Pharaoh and all who were in his house were struck with a plague. Everyone became ill except Sarah! The diviners came forward to reveal to Pharaoh that he was housing another man's wife. And before Sarah knew it, she was being whisked out of the palace and sent on her way along with her husband and all of the wealth they had acquired while in the land.

This was not the only time that Sarah was a tool in the midst of Abraham's bad decisions. And it was also not the last time that God rescued her from being caught in the middle of her husband's mistakes. Eight chapters later in the book of Genesis, Abraham once again lost his confidence in God's protection. Once again he told Abimelech, the reigning monarch of the country in which they dwelt, that Sarah was his sister. Once again the king took her and claimed her for his own. God did not take this lightly. He visited the king in a dream and told him that he was a dead man for taking Sarah, Abraham's wife. The king reasoned with God that he had not touched Sarah, but God was quick to point out to him that He was the one who had kept him from touching Sarah. In other words, don't be so quick to

---

Submission is a command to everyone, men and women alike. Until we see submission as God's instruction to become vulnerable enough to receive, we will fail to recognize that submission is an invitation to be blessed.

---

brag about being virtuous because you would have touched her if I had allowed it. God instructed the king to give Sarah back to Abraham, "quick and in a hurry," if he wanted to live. Then God promised to have Abraham pray for him because he was a prophet. That morning, the king called for Abraham and confronted him about his masquerade as Sarah's brother. After Abraham explained his fears, the king gave him livestock and servants along with a thousand pieces of silver and told him that they could live anywhere they liked. They were to have no more fear of him. Abraham then prayed for God to heal Abimelech's wife and maidservants, for He had closed up everybody's womb until Sarah's release. So all the women in King Abimelech's house became pregnant. And the anointing for fruitfulness spread even to Sarah. It was after this that Sarah also became pregnant.

Now, why did I take the time to retell that whole story? Because so many women struggle with the "s" word. You got it—we're getting ready to talk about submission! Because many women have partners who are not submitted to God, submission becomes an even more horrifying concept. I felt it was important to illustrate how faithfully God guards His women, even when the men who are supposed to be leading them guide them down the wrong path. This is why your house must be built with wisdom. I am not going to tell you to submit to abuse or other things that clearly violate the Word of God. But I am going to tell you that until you can bring yourself to trust God as your ultimate covering, even over that of your mate or whoever is your authority, you will have trouble in River City. For the unmarried, this applies to you as well. Your pastor, father, and employer are your authorities. You will yield to your mate whenever you receive him in the same respect that you yield to those I just stated. Submission is a command to everyone, men and women alike. Until we see submission as God's instruction to become vulnerable enough to receive, we will fail to recognize that submission is an invitation to be blessed.

The word "submission" is not synonymous with "doormat." Your cooperation is required in submission. You have to decide to go along with another person. Therefore, you are not rolling over; you have merely decided to walk in agreement. It takes strength to do that, especially if you're not quite sure you agree with the direction in which you're headed. Sarah's story proves this. In spite of Abraham's actions, God protected Sarah! He didn't allow Pharaoh or King Abimelech to touch her. Remember, King Abimelech thought he had done good not to touch her until God told him it wasn't that he had been good, it was the hand of God that kept him from violating Sarah. Though the going seemed a little hairy in both situations, Abraham and Sarah left richer because of Sarah. Thanks to God.

Now, why is it that Abraham could trust God enough to leave his home for parts unknown? Could believe God to give him a son in his old age? Could watch Him burn down the cities of Sodom and Gomorrah and deliver Lot, yet still not trust God to protect his wife? Because Sarah was just too precious to him. He couldn't bear the thought of the king killing him and taking his wife. The thought of her being forced to be the wife of a stranger, a godless man, was too much for Abraham to bear. He was not willing to take any chances with her life. Just as single women can believe God for everything except a mate and mothers can believe God for everything except the safety of their children, the same principle prevails here. We have trouble releasing our most precious things into the care of God. For some reason, we do not believe that what we view as precious is even more precious to God and that He is well able to keep those things we hold dear. How it wrenches our hearts when we have done everything we can think of, yet to no avail, and we are forced to release our dreams, our mates, and our children into the hands of God, stand still, and see His salvation.

God doesn't want us to work that hard only to fall prey to trauma; He simply wants us to submit. I'll tell you a little secret. If you can submit to the authority in your life, even when everything in you is screaming that this direction is not the wisest choice, God will give those in authority the grace to see their own mistakes. They'll love you more because you didn't point them out *and* they'll be more open to your counsel the next go-round. But if you dig in your heels and point out their stupidity, their only defense is to put on the muscle and force you to do what they've asked in order to prove and secure their own position. If it turns out to be a mess, they'll never admit that they made a mistake because you've already offended their sense of dignity. They now have no grace to see their faults, and you have become the fall guy in the whole fiasco. No one should ever feel they have to defend their point of view to you. They should always feel that they can ask for your suggestion without judgment.

Don't Stop the Flow

One day a woman came to Elisha the prophet. Her husband, who had worked for Elisha, had died. She was now left in debt to a creditor who had threatened to take her two sons for slaves as payment. Elisha asked her what she had in her house. (There's that "house" thing again.) The woman replied that all she had was a flask of olive oil. He then instructed her to borrow as many empty jars as she could from friends and neighbors. Then she was to go home, shut the door behind her, and pour the olive oil from the flask into the empty containers, setting them aside as they were filled. And the woman was obedient. She poured and poured until every container she had borrowed was filled. When she ran out of empty containers, the oil stopped flowing. She was then able to pay her debts.

Now, there are a couple of things here that are important to note in the area of submission. The woman had a need. She went to the prophet, who told her to do something. She didn't ask him why or stand there trying to figure it out; she did what he said—borrow empty vessels. Keep in mind that it is impossible to submit when you are full of yourself. Submission calls for you to be open to direction, emptying yourself of all your own ideas on the subject to make room for other possibilities. The next step is to close the door to your house behind you. After all, this submission thing is personal. It is between you, God, and your authority, whether that be your mate or your employer. It's not an open forum for everyone else to throw in their two cents worth. Submission will be easier for you if it is a private affair. Lots of times it is difficult to submit because you're too cognizant of what everyone else thinks about you submitting to your husband. Just remember, all those girlfriends who think it is ridiculous for you to listen to your husband go home either to empty homes or problems with their own mate. Don't believe the hype. At the end of the day, the widow had what she needed to pay her debt and enough left over for her and her sons to live on comfortably. And isn't that what it's really all about? It's about getting what you need and desire. You've got to give to get; there's no way around it. It's one of the rules of the kingdom.

When Abraham decided it was time for Isaac to be married, he sent his servant to find a bride from among his people. One of the stipulations was that she had to be willing to come to where Isaac was. The chosen woman, Rebekah, left where she was, followed a man she did not know, and ended up married to a wealthy man and became the mother of two nations. She could have put her hand on her hip and said, "Well, why can't *he* move *here?*" But she didn't. She submitted to the unknown in order to be blessed with a husband birthed from promise. Ruth submitted herself to her mother-in-law's instructions and laid down at a man's feet in order to be blessed with a wealthy husband and an entry into the lineage of Jesus Christ. Esther submitted herself in service to her king in order to be blessed with the preservation of her life and the life of her people. Are you seeing the pattern here?

Sometimes I think that the Word of God is just too easy for us. We want things to be more complicated than they really are so that we can believe we had a hand in the final outcome. When Naaman the army commander had leprosy, he was sent to Elisha to be healed. Elisha simply sent his servant out with a message that Naaman should dip himself in the Jordan seven times in order to be healed. Naaman was insulted. "Doesn't he know who I am? How dare he send some common servant out to give me a message to go and dunk myself in the dirtiest river in Israel? Doesn't he know he's supposed to do this thing right, in a manner befitting my station in life? He should have come out himself, waved his hand over me, called on the Lord with a great display, and healed me!" (That's Naaman quoted in Michelle paraphrase.) One of his officers tried to reason that if Elisha had told him to do something difficult in order to secure his healing, surely he would have done it. Therefore, why not try this simple thing? So Naaman went down to the Jordan River and dipped himself in it seven times. And you know what happened? He was completely cured.

What is the problem that we share with Naaman? The problem of pride and self-righteousness. These two friends can squeeze the life out of a blessing in no time. I get this picture of God saying, "Hey, you're so together. You got it covered, bless yourself." Why dip in a dirty river? Naaman needed to see just how dirty he really was. Not outside, but inside. He needed a revelation that he may be "the man" when it came to the army, but God was the ultimate man. He needed to submit to the knowledge of who he really was in God's sight before he could be healed. Some of us need to submit to the knowledge of what is really in our hearts before we can move to the next stage of blessing. Pride will keep you from coming clean with God. Self-righteousness will keep you from experiencing the flow of God's cleansing and liberating power. It is that power which enables us to submit to the wishes of men. If the words "I'm sorry, I was wrong," are words you find difficult to say while "I told you so," comes easily, consider the state of your heart. It is probably not ripe for submission and the blessings that come with it.

Did you know that God will allow those in authority to lean on you just to show you what's inside your heart?

> "The human heart is most deceitful and desperately wicked. Who really knows how bad it is? But I know! I, the LORD, search all hearts and examine secret motives. I give all people their due rewards, according to what their actions deserve" (Jeremiah 17:9,10 NLT).

> "Remember how the LORD your God led you through the wilderness for forty years, humbling you and testing you to prove your character, and to find out whether or not you would really obey his commands" (Deuteronomy 8:2 NLT).

"The LORD your God will drive those nations out ahead of you little by little. You will not clear them away all at once, for if you did, the wild animals would multiply too quickly for you" (Deuteronomy 7:22 NLT).

Too much freedom given too quickly, before we've mastered the art of submission, leaves us vulnerable for the "wild beasts" of excess and lack of discipline to devour us. It's like a poor person winning a large sum of money. Often the money is soon spent because the person wasn't prepared to deal with it properly. He or she had no prior experience dealing with sizable finances. Even Jesus had to submit. He submitted to separation from His heavenly Father unto death in order to gain the blessing of all of us being delivered from sin, liberated to become His bride. He, too, had to learn obedience through the things that He suffered (Hebrews 5:8).

Speaking of Jesus, let's talk about Mary, His mother. The hot new phrase on the street in response to "How are you?" is "Blessed and highly favored!" But let's take a closer look at those words. This is not a sentence to fling around lightly. How does one qualify for blessing and favor? How did Mary qualify? Don't you assume that God did an in-depth character study before selecting the mother for His only begotten Son? After all, every woman in Israel dreamed of being the mother of the Redeemer. So how did Mary win the coveted title? What was it about her that made her so special to God? First of all, Mary was submitted, completely yielded and available to God. When the angel told her that she would bear a son and explained to her how it would happen without the help of a natural man, Mary's response was, "I am the Lord's servant. May it be to me as you have said" (Luke 1:38 NIV). Another translation says, "I am the Lord's *slave*" (emphasis added). That's how yielded she was. No ego stood between her and God. She simply believed Him and yielded to His word. When she went to visit her cousin Elizabeth with the news of her pregnancy, Elizabeth told Mary that she was blessed because she believed God's promises.

Mary was also blessed and highly favored because she did not fear man's opinion of her obedience to God. Mary's pregnancy could have gotten her in big trouble. She was a single woman betrothed, or engaged, to Joseph. She was not yet joined with him in matrimony; therefore, she could have been accused of adultery. Let's get real here. How many people were going to be open to the concept that she had conceived of the Holy Ghost? Even Joseph couldn't quite swallow that at first. He thought to quietly put her away so she wouldn't be stoned to death, until the angel confirmed the story. From this story, you can see that it doesn't pay to fear man's opinion and ignore God's direction.

Not long ago I saw an article in a well-known women's magazine that caught my eye. In the article, one of the interviewees said that God had forced Himself on Mary, taken her womb, and done as He pleased with it. I was highly offended by this person's gross misjudgment of God's character, as well as the obvious error in reference to the Scriptures. God is a gentleman. He woos us to His side. He invites us to come and sit at His table. Before the beginning of time, He knew how each heart would respond to Him, and He regulated His purposes accordingly. He knew that Mary would be willing. Her willingness, mixed with other wonderful traits of character that she possessed, earned her an appointment with God that would change the course of the world. No, there was no coercion present in this matter. This is the reason why submission is even an issue—it must be voluntary. God isn't about to force anyone to do anything. That would be going against His own Word, which He cannot do. He has made us all free agents. If God were in the business of wringing our arms behind our backs and forcing us to do exactly as He pleased, we would not even be examining the topic of submission. Submission is not only a test of our love for Him, it is a test of our strength. Sometimes it is hard to submit, but submit we must. Why? Because it is always in our best interest to do so, regardless of what our eyes seem to see or how much we think we know.

I find it interesting to note that Mary had a full understanding of this. After she married Joseph, God gave *Joseph*—not Mary—the directions concerning what they should do. It was to *Joseph* that instruction was given to go down to Egypt to protect the life of the Christ child. It was to *Joseph* that the word was given when to return. What if Mary had gotten an attitude, done a sister-girl neck roll, and said, "Now, looka here! I just had the Son of God! I think I hear from God, too, and He didn't tell me to go anywhere. I want to take my baby home for my friends and family to see." She could have claimed to have more experience with God, more spiritual sensitivity. But she didn't do that. She submitted to her husband's leadership. As she yielded to his lead, their lives were preserved and her Son was lifted up for all the world to see.

So let's get this straight. When the Lord spoke to Mary, He also spoke to her fiancé to confirm what He had told her. But when He spoke to Joseph, He did not backtrack to Mary to qualify what He had said. I think I'll just leave that one hanging in the air for a moment. Kinda makes you go hmm, doesn't it?

On second thought, I'd better clarify this point for those of you who would like to claim amnesia in the understanding department. When God speaks a word to a woman, He will confirm it in the spirit of the person in authority over you. Now, you might be one of those ultrasensitive-in-the-spirit folks who gets messages from God way in advance. Just because your mate, your boss, or your pastor hasn't gotten the message yet doesn't mean they can't hear God. It might be a timing thing. Remember, Joseph had a dream about something that didn't happen for years. His family couldn't see it at the time he shared it with them, but it most certainly came to pass according to God's appointed timetable. So that man's inability to hear what you're hearing may be God using him to slow you down until it's really time to run with the plan He's given you. Sometimes we women talk entirely too much. We drown out the voice of the Holy Spirit. When we get a word or a revelation from God, we need to learn how to birth that thing in prayer until those in authority hear from God themselves and come to us to share what they've heard. Then they'll be ready to assist us rather than tightening our reins. This is not a contest, so there is no need to claim the credit for hearing it first.

Last but not least, Mary had to ultimately submit to her own Son, and then submit—or release—her Son back to God. Her entire life was a testament to the blessing of submission—to God, to His divine purposes, to her mate, to her Son. Single and married women alike should be encouraged by this. God wants to birth Jesus in every single one of you. He wants you to bear gifts, namely the fruit of the Spirit, to the world that change the courses of the lives around you, but this will only come to fruition as you submit. Then you, too, will be blessed and highly favored. Though God gives some blessings for free, do not be deceived—not all blessings come without cost. Some special ones come wrapped in favor paper, and these are expensive. They cost your willingness to live a submitted life on every level.

A Time to Speak and a Time to Be Silent

"So does this mean that women just walk around never voicing an opinion about anything, Michelle?" you may ask. I hear you, I hear you. Of course not, silly! There's a time for everything. The time to speak is when the Lord tells you to speak. When He says, "Tell it," He will have your back. The story of Bathsheba comes to mind here. As I shared with you in an earlier chapter, David was dying and one of his other sons had taken over the throne. Nathan the prophet came to Bathsheba and told her she needed to speak with David immediately. She needed to put him in remembrance of his promise that Solomon would be the one to succeed him on the throne. Nathan told her when to go and said that he would show up while she was still speaking with the king to confirm what she was saying. And so she went, knowing she didn't have to hit David over the head with a hammer because God was behind her. She gently reminded David of his promise, and while she was still speaking, Nathan showed up to reinforce what she was saying. David then made sure the matter was taken care of right away.

In the thirteenth chapter of Judges, the angel of the Lord appeared to Samson's mother, giving her personal instructions for the Nazarite son she was about to bear. When she went to tell her husband what had happened, he then prayed and asked God to return with further instructions on how to care for the child. The Lord honored his prayer and returned

to confirm what his wife had told him. Once again, this illus-
trates that God will back up a woman when He has given her
a word to speak. Women need to pray for the sensitivity of
their men to the Spirit of God. The more men grasp the
reality of God speaking to them, the more they will respect
you when you come bearing a word from the Lord.

Elizabeth's husband, Zechariah, was visited by the angel of
the Lord and told that his wife would become pregnant with
John the Baptist. Because he and Elizabeth were well down
the road in years, Zechariah couldn't believe it. The angel
told him that he would not be able to speak again until the
day the promise came to pass. Immediately Zechariah was
struck dumb. Elizabeth became pregnant and had the baby,
just as the angel Gabriel had said. When asked what she
would name the baby, Elizabeth told the people, "John." The
people disagreed, voicing their opinion that the child should
be named after his father. Upon seeking her husband's
counsel, Elizabeth was backed up when Zechariah wrote the
name "John" on a tablet. Immediately his mouth was opened,
and he began praising God.

What's the moral of the story? Though in this case, the
angel did not go to Elizabeth but rather to her husband,
there's still something to be learned here. When Zechariah
could not believe the word of the Lord concerning his wife,
the Lord shut his mouth. The Lord is well able to put the
man in your life under arrest if he hinders God's move in
your life with his actions or words of unbelief. It is not your
job to convince him of what God said or to talk down to him
when he doesn't get it. There's no need to tell him he needs
to get saved or become spiritually deeper. If it was God who
spoke to you, He is able to follow through on His own word
and do whatever it takes to bring that man into agreement

while He brings His word to fruition. You simply need to remain in the right attitude of graciousness and let God fix the situation for you. To move ahead of that man's agreement will set you up for deception and all sorts of trouble. God will now have to stop what He's doing and fix you because you're out of order. You can end up holding up your own blessing, so be sure to stay in the right attitude.

When God tells you to speak, He has no problem being your enforcer. You won't have to demand your way. You can simply and sweetly make your request known like Esther did and watch that man move mountains on your behalf. I recall that a gentleman friend of mine always said to me, "Whenever I ask you to do something and you so sweetly go along with what I say, it does something to my heart. It makes me want to just shower you with everything you want! You are such a woman. I really like that." At the time I didn't understand why this was such a big deal to him, but I do now. I never made him feel threatened or condemned by my attitude. I trusted him to see the error of his own ways, encouraging him in failure and celebrating his victories. He felt safe to learn in front of me because I never stripped him of his manhood in the process. He felt that I trusted him to hear God's leading. I allowed him to experience whatever he needed to experience within the realm of his own personal journey so that he could grow. I gave him the room to do that just as I would for any of my female friends. We all deserve to be given that type of respect. We don't always know every detail of what God is trying to work out in those around us. Therefore, we need to get out of the way and let Him do His thing.

Of course, I must address here two of the most poorly-interpreted Scriptures of all time. You know the ones—the ones about women being silent in the church. Let's look at them carefully together, shall we?

> "For God is not a God of disorder but of peace. As in all the congregations of the saints, women should remain silent in the churches. They are not allowed to speak, but must be in submission, as the Law says. If they want to inquire about something, they should ask their own husbands at home; for it is disgraceful for a woman to speak in the church" (1 Corinthians 14:33-35 NIV).

> "A woman should learn in quietness and full submission. I do not permit a woman to teach or to have authority over a man; she must be silent. For Adam was formed first, then Eve. And Adam was not the one deceived; it was the woman who was deceived and became a sinner" (1 Timothy 2:11-14 NIV).

Now, now, ladies, calm down! I'm getting ready to fix this for you. Let us look at the context of Paul's statement. He had just finished giving the Corinthian church a rundown on orderly conduct during their services. He had found that everyone was talking all over one another. Everyone had a prophecy, a song, a revelation, a tongue, an interpretation, an instruction. Everyone was so excited about all these new spiritual gifts and revelations they were having that they were being downright rude to one another! The women, who had not been formally trained in matters of the Bible up to this point, were thrilled to finally be let into this arena. They were excited, too. As they learned they realized that they had things to share along with a lot of questions. In addition to this, many of the women were beginning to challenge the men as they grasped this new information. Keep in mind that in Corinthian society, women had not been allowed to confront men in public. Now, finally, they were free. But those still new in their faith found it disconcerting to see women asking questions and challenging some of the teachings. Therefore, Paul told the women to ask these questions at home and to not take advantage of their new freedom so as not to cause consternation among those who weren't yet grounded in the faith.

As for the second passage, again I must clarify that Paul was speaking about a specific church that was having a lot of trouble. The Ephesian church had a problem with an influx of false teachers. The women of the church seemed to be most susceptible to the false teachings because they had not yet acquired enough Bible knowledge to be able to discern the truth. At this point, they were all baby Christians who had not been privy to studying the Scriptures before now. Yet here they were challenging those who had been studying for years and in some cases were promoting false teachers and revelations that were in error! The men had a jump start on them (mirroring the order of creation—Adam first, then Eve, who was deceived); therefore, the women needed to sit down and learn from those who were qualified to teach them without disputing what they heard. A little bit of knowledge can be dangerous. These women needed to acquire the full truth along with understanding, experience, and Christian maturity. The word "silent" here in the Greek expresses an attitude of quietness and composure. A different word is used to communicate complete silence. These women also seemed to be having an issue about wearing inappropriate clothing. This was a situation where abuses of new freedom were abundant and had to be corrected. This increasingly became a problem across the board as churches began to spring up, causing this to become a universal mandate to women everywhere. Therefore, Paul was instructing Timothy not to put any of the women in leadership positions because of their inexperience and susceptibility to deception.

Everyone was clamoring for leadership positions in the Ephesian church, so Paul took the time to lay out the requirements for all of them everywhere. Based on their behavior, he made it painstakingly clear—even with the men—that Christian maturity, sound moral character, and a pure and blameless life coupled with great faith and sound doctrine were requirements that could not be negotiated.

Paul was noway, nohow, saying that women should not be allowed to speak in church. How could he when earlier in the same letter to the Corinthians, giving instruction for public worship, he addressed the matter of women praying and prophesying in public?

> "And every woman who prays or prophesies with her head uncovered dishonors her head—it is just as though her head were shaved. If a woman does not cover her head, she should have her hair cut off; and if it is a disgrace for a woman to have her hair cut or shaved off, she should cover her head....For this reason, and because of the angels, the woman ought to have a sign of authority on her head" (1 Corinthians 11:5,6,10 NIV).

Let's face it—she wasn't prophesying to herself. So you tell me what's going on here. Does Paul really instruct women to cover their heads as a sign that they are under authority when they pray and prophesy in public, and then turn around and tell them not to speak in church? I don't think so! Paul knew too many women holding substantial positions in churches to have this type of attitude. If these women were doing anything responsible, they had to interact with and relegate to men as well as women. We know that Priscilla, along with her husband, Aquila, taught Apollos. Phoebe was a deaconess. Mary, Tryphena, and Tryphosa labored hard for the Lord. Euodia and Syntyche worked side by side with Paul, contending for the faith.

The note I must make here is that all of these women in leadership positions had a visible authority to whom they were in submission. They were not just hanging out in the wind, running off to minister uncovered. Even I am under the authority of my pastor as I travel and speak. To go out uncovered would be dangerous. When I make a break-through in spiritual understanding in a certain area, I run it by my pastor and other mature men in Christ to make sure I have received the understanding in balance and harmony with the Scriptures. I check and cross-check before I go sprinting off to deliver the Word, no matter how wonderful it might sound to me. Remember, women are the ones the serpent targets first for deception because of the power of influence we possess. Remember when God appointed Deborah as judge over Israel? She was still a woman in submission. But this brings up another interesting point. Would God place a woman as leader of a nation, then ban women from speaking in church? This would be a great contradiction. No, God has given women too much to say, too many incredible revelations to share, to subject them to silence.

I must interject here that women can deliver everything that God has given them to deliver while still maintaining their femininity. We are not to "dress" like men, in the sense of feeling that we have to be like men when we get up to deliver a message. We have our own unique way of serving things up that is extremely effective. There is no need for you to feel that you have to outpreach a man, or even preach like a man. You must simply give the Word. When the food is good, people eat. In this no one is offended. Paul was merely saying that at the end of the day, it was crucial that

You cannot be feminine in this world unless you completely understand how covered by God you are. Then you will no longer react to men, but respond to His voice.

women remained under the protective covering of authority even in this area. So let's not blame unclear understanding or, in some cases, overblown egos on Paul. This is the same Paul who said that there was no male or female, Greek or Jew, okay? Women were free to lift up the body with the gifts God had given them, in an orderly fashion. However, they were not to challenge the men in public or teach others when they had not acquired enough knowledge to do an effective job. There is a time and a place for everything in order to keep the peace. That doesn't even have to be straight from the Bible. It just makes good sense.

So when should you be silent? You should be silent when you differ with a man in a public setting, or when your disagreement makes that man vulnerable to ruin or disgrace before his peers and family. This should apply to anyone, male or female. However, there is nothing more degrading and pathetic than when a woman goes off on a man and embarrasses him in public. No one likes to see a henpecked man or a man disgraced by a woman in a crowd. In the book of Esther, Queen Vashti did just that. Now, before all of you who think that Queen Vashti was right begin to protest, let me have my say. I understand that the tradition of the day was on her side. A woman was not to show herself to men in public the way her husband wanted her to show herself. I know that he was drunk and therefore considered to be out of his mind when he made the request. I know that Vashti recognized his request as a serious breach of protocol and refused to go on principle. I know all of that, *but*—and that is a resounding *but*—Vashti was wrong. She was right in motive, but wrong in action. This is what separates the unfeminine women from the feminine women. You cannot be feminine in this world unless you completely understand how covered by God you are. Then you will no longer react to men, but respond to His voice.

You will master the art of timing, speech, inflection, movement—you name it, it all plays a part in the bottom-line resolution to a situation.

Knowing how protective God is of women, I can say beyond a shadow of a doubt that if Vashti had donned her royal robes and made her way to the palace out of obedience to her husband, something would have happened to save her from disgracing herself. Someone would have spoken some sense into the king, he would have had a moment of remorse, a fire would have broken out at the party and dispersed the crowd...*something!* God can use anything, and something surely would have happened. So though Vashti went for honor, she *dishonored* her husband and was dethroned. She demanded respect and was banished from those from whom she demanded it. She was the queen. She was the trendsetter for all the women of the country. The men were not having it. They were not going to go home to wives who would now feel that if the queen got away with such obvious, blatant disrespect, they could, too. Though God used the whole situation to put Esther in place to save a nation, Vashti seriously missed the point. The issue went far beyond her personal world. It affected the kingdom.

> "Everyone must submit [themselves] to the governing authorities, for there is no authority except that which God has established. The authorities that exist have been established by God. Consequently, he who rebels against the authority is rebelling against what God has instituted, and those who do so will bring judgment on themselves. For rulers hold no terror for those who do right, but for those who do wrong. Do you want to be free from fear of the one in authority? Then do what is right and he will commend you....Therefore, it is necessary to submit to the authorities, not only because of possible punishment but also because of conscience" (Romans 13:1-3,5 NIV).

> "Obey your leaders and submit to their authority. They keep watch over you as men who must give an

account. Obey them so that their work will be a joy, not a burden, for that would be of no advantage to you" (Hebrews 13:17 NIV).

"Submit yourselves for the Lord's sake to every authority instituted among men: whether to the king, as the supreme authority, or to governors, who are sent by him to punish those who do wrong and to commend those who do right. For it is God's will that by doing good you should silence the ignorant talk of foolish men....Live as servants of God. Show proper respect to everyone" (1 Peter 2:13-17 NIV).

Well, you could say that the king and Vashti were both ungodly people. The king was not spiritually sensitive. He would not have been open to God's correction. God was able to get this same king up early one morning to bring to his attention that he had not rewarded Mordecai for uncovering a plot against his life. God was able to arrest this same king from handing down a death sentence when Esther did the opposite of Vashti, violating his law and appearing to him when she had not been bidden. So while you're worrying about some little ole man, don't tell me who's really in control.

"The king's heart is in the hand of the LORD; he directs it like a watercourse wherever he pleases" (Proverbs 21:1 NIV).

"In his heart a man plans his course, but the LORD determines his steps" (Proverbs 16:9 NIV).

"Many are the plans in a man's heart, but it is the LORD's purpose that prevails" (Proverbs 19:21 NIV).

So there! Anyone still think you have to arm wrestle and grow hair on your chest in order to have your say? I think not. Just remember, when you walk in submission, the person who is your covering is held responsible for you. If you walk out from under that covering, you are the one who will get wet. I love walking down the street next to a good, old-fashioned man. He always walks on the outside. If your position shifts when you turn the corner, he politely guides you back to the inside of the sidewalk. Why? So that if a passing vehicle splashes up water, he will be the one who gets wet instead of you. That's the idea of submission. He should get wet, not you.

I realize that you have been doing things your own way for a long time, and though you are weary, letting go is a scary proposition. But let go you must. Let go of the reins. Let go of the idea that you must control everything in your world or nothing will happen. Let go of the concept that you have to be tough in order to gain respect and influence people. It's just not true. You can be your soft, warm, wise, feminine self and still get everything accomplished. Appeal to the heart of the one in authority, don't demand. As a matter of fact, the more feminine you are, the more assistance you will get from the men. Your work will be cut in half! Have you ever noticed how quickly men will turn into a pile of mush and sheepishly grin when you tell them how they saved your day? Try it sometime; you'll be amazed. Men are like little boys just waiting for a word of appreciation. It literally makes them strut and bend over backwards to do more. So let God throw His weight around while you just keep doing what you do best—being all woman.

"Wives, submit to your husbands as to the Lord. For the husband is head of the wife as Christ is the head of the church, his body, of which he is the Savior. Now as the church submits to Christ, so also wives should submit to their husbands in everything" (Ephesians 5:22-24 NIV).

There is a little proverb in Africa that goes something like this: "The man is the head, the woman is the neck, and wherever the neck turns, the head turns." The neck doesn't scream and shout, doesn't put up a fuss; it just ever so gently...turns. And the head goes with it. Now, the head is extremely important. It houses the brain, which tells the rest of the body what to do. When someone is brain-dead, everything comes to a screeching halt. The rest of the body can't function. The head is the source of productivity for all of the other limbs. It sits above them and covers them all. The neck is definitely underneath the head. It carries the head and encircles the spine, which encases the spinal cord, which is your nerve center, responsible for making you feel things! Now, if your neck gets broken, that means death because the connection between the head and the body—where the other vital organs reside—has been severed. So though the neck may look unimportant, nothing could be further from the truth. And let's face it, the neck gets to sport a lot of fabulous jewelry.

As we consider the connection of the head to the rest of the body, a natural illustration comes to mind. Many a man has been changed and made socially presentable because of a woman. The truth of the matter is, no part is less important than the other, but by working together all are made strong. The phrase "The head of the woman is the man," is not about supremacy. It is an indication that the man is to be the source of the woman. After all, woman was taken out of man, the source of her existence, just as man is from Christ and Christ is from God. No kitchen can be filled with many cooks all dipping into the same pot and expect to have anything less than a mess as a result of the chaos. You can't get anything done with all chiefs and no Indians. Someone has to cast the decisive vote. Authority bears responsibility. This is the boundary that forces the one in authority to make good choices for all involved. Authority makes things run smoothly. Submission makes them run even smoother. It is not a matter of inferior versus superior; it is simply a matter of order and function. Jesus, though equal with God, submitted to God the Father in order to save us all. And that's the bottom line. Submission is mutual commitment and cooperation to achieve the greater end. And that, my friend, is much greater than all of us.

"Submit to one another out of reverence for Christ" (Ephesians 5:21 NIV).

Dear Heavenly Father, thank You for being my covering. As I rest beneath Your care, help me to keep my faith focused on You and not on the weakness of the arm of flesh. As my knowledge of You grows, strengthen my capacity to yield to authority, keeping in mind that in actuality I am yielding to You. As I am tempted to go my own way, do my own thing, and take matters into my own hands, grant me a revelation of

You sitting on the throne, still in control of every area of my life. Help me to rest in the knowledge of Your care for me. Increase my trust in You to break my fall when others let me down. As I look to You to be my rear guard, to instruct me when to speak and when to be silent, please show up on my behalf. And in the times when I hold my peace, grant me a visitation of Your Spirit to assuage my fears. Lord, I want to be the woman You have called me to be, completely available and yielded to You, to Your direction, for the completion of Your purposes and Your ultimate glory. Lord, here am I, an empty vessel. Come and fill me with Yourself as I surrender my all to You. In Jesus' name. Amen.

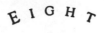

EIGHT

The
Power
of
Influence

She spun her web
    carefully
  methodically
     artistically
      entrapping his mind
         watching him flail in indecision
      pulled between his own instincts
        and her suggestions
           he tossed amidst the silky threads
            that grew tighter
              with every inner protest
     and she
   watching from afar
    gazed at her creation
     trusting that he would see
       the wisdom of her words soon enough
and just as she thought it time to move in
       and claim her prizes
     her foot became caught in her own snare
      crying out for help
    she realized too late
      the help she sought was also entrapped
        rendered useless by her own hands
     gazing at one another
       across the distance of their predicament
      they watched one another
          die separate deaths
   slowly
    painfully
  amidst misunderstandings
  and a million regrets

he
    for not being strong enough
        to keep her from her own ruin
she
    for not letting go of the reins
        and grasping his hands instead
           his hands
                that now seemed further away than ever
       constrained by her own determinations
         losing the power they once had...
    feeling her own strength dissipating
         as she watched the color drain from his fingertips
she realized all too late
    that webs of manipulation
        though beautiful in the making
           were the most deceptive of all
    their delicate lattice work
        quickly transforming into iron prisons
           that bound both
               "victor" and victim
    the chasm of betrayal
        too broad to afford
    them the comfort of one another's solace
        as they quietly died inside
           too tired to fight
    too ashamed of their own participation
        in this most shameful demise
they closed their eyes
    and dreamed of better days
        as she concluded
           that webs were best left
                to the work of spiders...

*H*erodias paced back and forth across the floor of her chambers, her agitation growing with each step. The harsh impact of her shoes on the tiles, resounding to the outer corridor, only heightened the angry cadence of her heart—but not enough to drown out the words of John the Baptist. His strident voice proclaiming her sins for all to hear practically drove her to madness. Why her husband, Herod, wouldn't silence him once and for all was beyond her. Herod actually was intrigued by what this so-called prophet had to say! She was not amused. She did not relish the thought of hearing how dreadful it was for Herod to take her from his own brother. If he thought she had been placated by his imprisonment, she most certainly had not! She bit her bottom lip thoughtfully and her eyes scoured the room, as if seeking some solution from among the folds of the rich tapestries that draped the interior. She had to find a way to convince Herod to have that man executed. She wanted him dead. Anything short of this was unacceptable. Perhaps by the end of dinner, when Herod's spirits had been lifted by wine, she could find a way to coax him into granting her strongest desire.

Herod was indeed in high spirits that evening. Herodias watched his eyes lustfully wander toward her daughter more than once as the evening matured. If Herod thought that she, Herodias, would allow herself to be replaced by her own daughter, he had another thing coming. But as she watched this subtle undercurrent flow throughout the evening, a plan formed in her mind. No, she would not be replaced by her daughter, but she most certainly would not be above using her daughter to get what she wanted. She knew Herod. She knew what he liked. She knew that he made rash promises when he was inebriated. This collection of facts was enough for her to formalize her scheme. She gestured for her daughter to draw close, then whispered a suggestion into her ear.

She had been trained well, Herodias thought, as she watched her daughter dance before the king. Even now, a glaze was coming across Herod's eyes as his eyelids grew heavy with desire. Sensing the intensity of Herodias' gaze upon him, he snapped out of his lascivious stupor to proclaim that he was so pleased with the performance that he would give his stepdaughter up to half the kingdom. What would she have? So she, having been previously prompted by her mother, replied, "The head of John the Baptist." There! It was done! Where there is a will, there is a way to get what you want.

How was Herodias to know that silencing the voice of one man would never silence her own desperate spirit? Though John the Baptist was now dead, her guilt was still alive and well. Many more sleepless nights would she spend pacing back and forth in her chambers, wrestling with demons that were far more frightening than the accusations of the late prophet, for the condemnation of sin has a life of its own.

The gift of influence is the invisible power that women overlook.

The Way of a Woman

Who can say when it really starts? I've watched my five-month-old niece completely wrap her father around her finger with one gorgeous smile. A grown man turns to mush before my very eyes, and I think to myself, "Something's going on here." Boy, if I could bottle this magic, I would be a rich woman! Is this power we possess inherently part of who we are as women? Is it part of our nature via the fall? Or is it taught? Without speaking a word, the iron will of a man melts away. With one glance, a whole room stops. One touch has sent armies to war. A woman's influence can make or break a man. It can turn the tide of a nation's destiny. After all the atrocities of segregation, it was a lovely little woman sitting on a bus who catapulted the civil rights movement into action. Why? Because influence is more powerful than authority.

How can that be? Because influence is a heart thing. Think about it this way. A cop can stand in the middle of the road and put his hand up for cars to stop, and they comply. Why? Because people know that the cop is an authority figure. They respect his office, so they yield to his authority. He does not have the *physical* power to stop the cars, but he does have the *positional* authority to bring them to a halt. However, if someone in one of those cars decided they didn't feel like stopping, it would take the influence of someone to convince them otherwise. Get the difference?

The gift of influence is the invisible power that women overlook—the ability to affect the heart of a man in order to change his mind. The heart is the originator of all decisions.

> "For as he thinks in his heart, so is he" (Proverbs 23:7 NKJV).

> "As water reflects a face, so a man's heart reflects the man" (Proverbs 27:19 NIV).

> "The good man brings good things out of the good stored up in his heart, and the evil man brings evil things out of the evil stored up in his heart. For out of the overflow of his heart his mouth speaks" (Luke 6:45 NIV).

Influence is overlooked because we are credit-mongers by nature. If we could just get over the need to claim the credit for everything that takes place, we would be able to achieve more than we ever dreamed. If we could stop arguing over titles, we would see our wishes fulfilled and reap appropriate recompense and appreciation. When we free people to make their own choice to acknowledge us, it releases them to render praise. No farmer manipulates the ground until the seed he planted breaks through the soil and bears fruit. He plants the seed, lovingly waters it, gives it time and air to do its thing, and voilà! In the right season, the fruit bursts forth—the fruit he wanted! Others partake and are blessed by it, praising him for planting a good crop. And so it is with the heart of man or anyone we choose to influence. We must be willing to lovingly plant the right things in the heart, nourish the spirit without pressure, and then stand back and see the right decisions burst forth from that person. Isn't that what you *really* want?

Unfortunately, all of the wrong people seem to have grasped the power of this secret weapon of influence, and the gift has been misused. Influence at no time should overstep its boundaries and manifest itself in the form of manipulation. Herodias manipulated Herod to get what she wanted. Originally, Herod was not willing to kill John the Baptist. As a matter of fact, he only imprisoned him in the first place to placate Herodias. He did not like what John was saying, but he was willing to give him credit for being a prophet of God. He had enough good sense to know that you don't go messing with a man of God. Now Herod was in a fix. He had made a loud and extravagant promise to give the daughter of Herodias whatever she wanted. He could not rescind his promise in front of all the people. The Bible says that Herod was sorry he had to kill John the Baptist. He was trapped by his own wife.

Even worse, Herodias not only used her own daughter to get what she wanted, but she also taught her daughter how to be a manipulator. This was not setting the groundwork for a healthy relationship between them. The manipulated always become embittered toward the manipulators because the manipulated always come out the losers. After getting the head of John the Baptist for her mother, what did the daughter have to show for herself? She had blown her whole wad on something her mother wanted. So momma was happy, but what about daughter? She could have walked away with a new wardrobe, some beautiful jewelry, a parcel of land—something she could treasure for years to come. But, no, all she had was a bloody head on a platter that no one wanted to keep. And so it is with manipulation. The end result is usually a wash. No one ends up with anything lasting for themselves in the long run. After Herodias got her coveted head, do you think she felt any better? Of course not. She now had the blood of John the Baptist on her hands on top of all the other things she was battling. There is no winner in this story. "To obey is better than sacrifice, and to hearken than the fat of rams. For rebellion is as the sin of witchcraft, and stubbornness is as...idolatry" (1 Samuel 15:22,23 KJV).

Manipulation is likened to witchcraft, and God will never bless it because manipulation is an attempt to control through soulish means someone or something over which you don't have authority. Manipulation strikes at the heart of man through intimidation or seduction, thus coercing subjects to respond according to your desire and against their will. Rebellion and witchcraft run with the same bedfellows—debauchery, idolatry, hatred, discord, jealousy, fits of rage, selfish ambition, dissensions, factions, envy, drunkenness, orgies, and the like (Galatians 5:20). All are works of the flesh. Witchcraft is compared to rebellion because it forces someone to bend to another person's will other than God's. If the desire of your heart is truly of God, He is well able to birth agreement in the other person's spirit. For you to set up circumstances, manipulating situations to get your way, is only a clear indication that either your desire is not of God or it is not yet time for your wish to be granted. To move ahead of God always creates problems only seen in hindsight.

Oh, What a Tangled Web We Weave...

In order to understand how much God despises manipulation and to realize the curses that come upon our lives when we choose to operate in this fashion, let's take a look at good ole Queen Jezebel. She is the personification of manipulation. She would make manipulation look good if the end of the matter weren't so bad. We would all high-five one another and say she was a bad ma'ama-jamah for getting her man what he wanted, if only she hadn't been so deceitful. People got hurt. People died! And the judgment of God fell upon her house. All because girlfriend got a little too busy for all who were involved.

You know the story. Once upon a time there was a man named Naboth who had a vineyard near the palace. Jezebel's husband, Ahab, decided that he would like to have this field in order to extend his grounds, so he made Naboth an offer. Naboth declined the offer because the vineyard was the inheritance of his family. It was to be passed down through the generations; therefore, it was literally against the law of God for him to sell ancestral grounds. This he explained to Ahab, but Ahab cared nothing for the law of God. He went off to pout because he couldn't have his way. When Jezebel noticed his despondent countenance, she questioned his attitude, and Ahab in turn told her about his exchange with Naboth. She found his response pathetic at best. But a woman with a manipulative spirit thrives on the helplessness of men. This is an open door for her to rise to the occasion and take control. Masking her disdain, Jezebel assured her husband he should not worry his little royal head any further; she would take care of it. And take care of it she did. She wrote a letter in her husband's name, using his seal, ordering that a day of fasting be declared. Naboth was to be seated prominently at the gathering. Two scoundrels would then accuse him of cursing God and the king, which would lead to his stoning. This was carried out right away. And Jezebel calmly announced to the king that he could go and claim his silly little vineyard because Naboth was dead.

You know, I just have to break this down. It's filled with too many delicious little morsels. Jezebel makes modern-day divas of evil look like chopped liver. First of all, let's talk about her husband. Ahab was a wimp. An evil wimp, but a wimp just the same. Come on, the Bible says he went to his room and *pouted* after Naboth refused his offer. Even Jezebel couldn't believe it. Her attitude was, well, who is the king around here? Him or you? Usually a woman with a manipulative spirit has no respect for the person she decides to "help." In her mind, she now has to clean up another mess that this idiot has made. But she secretly likes to see the person down-and-out. She will even go so far as to plant seeds of disrespect in the hearts of others around the person in order to secure her position as controller. She will destroy the reputation of her husband to clear the path for herself. It is in this atmosphere that she can set herself up as the rescuer. She likes to look as if she saved the day. This builds feelings of dependency. No one would dare replace her, even if they

THE POWER OF FEMININITY

couldn't stand her, because she's convinced them that they
need her in order to function.

With this groundwork laid, she meticulously does her
dirty work beneath a cloak of behind-the-scenes deception.
She will use the name of the person she is "helping" to further her agenda. This ensures that the fallout doesn't fall
back on her. She plants her seeds of dissension well, waters
them with promises of reward or threats of retribution
(whichever work best), and sits back to view the final outcome. When the explosion comes, she wipes off her hands,
stifles a yawn, and moves on...*next!*

How does this manage to roam undetected in circles
where one would expect people to be more discerning?
Because the woman with a manipulative spirit is usually good
at mastering the outer traits of femininity as well as a very
convincing show of being religious. She surrounds herself
with false prophets, those who will speak what she wants to
hear. She is intimate with her select group of cronies, or so
they are led to believe. But she is always in control of how
close they really get to her because their presence is only
convenient as long as they carry out her wishes. This is why
Jezebel was furious when Elijah killed all of her prophets. She
could not believe that her little elves were all gone! They
had assisted her in leading her husband astray into Baal worship. This was the completion of his abdication from his role
as a husband. He was no longer priest, she was. And in that
position she could urge him to do all manner of evil because
he had submitted himself to her spiritual leadership. Now,
Baal can represent all forms of idolatry or materialism. When
a woman makes a man feel that he has to deliver all sorts of
things he can't afford in order to win that woman's respect,

he will eventually be led into dishonest means so that he can acquire all she desires.

Notice that Jezebel was not against praying, fasting, or taking part in any other outward religious shows. These things only heightened her reputation for possessing great spirituality, when in essence she hated all of these things in their pure form. She hated the true prophet of God, Elijah. She wanted him silenced. He was messing up her agenda of deception. She'd had everyone where she wanted them—until he came along. Her husband didn't give her a hard time because he feared her rage when she became upset. So he walked in agreement with her just to keep the peace. Anyone know any husbands like that? She even threw Elijah off for a minute when she threatened to kill him. Poor man, he had just finished calling down fire from heaven and killing 900 of Jezebel's prophets, and one threat from her sent him running. That type of caustic spirit will humble even the boldest man of God. The spirit of manipulation feels justified in all that it does.

And let's not forget that the manipulative woman is not above using her feminine wiles. She will pretty herself up with the best of them. Jezebel threw lavish banquets for her prophet cronies. She knew that the way to a man's heart is through his stomach. She covered all her bases, let me tell you. You don't think she had 900 prophets wrapped around her finger for nothing, do you? She was attractive, seductive, and she knew how to work a man if she must. Above all, she had no morals. Look again at the list of sins that accompany manipulation—sexual immorality, drunkenness, debauchery, impurity, and orgies. In its ceremonies, Baal worship included orgies as well as all the rest of the things on the list.

You might say that no one does this in the present day, but consider anything in excess as an orgy—a gorging of one's senses, so to speak. Even if it's not totally carried out, having an air of lasciviousness and using improper displays of sensuality to entice men to bend to your wishes falls into the same category. The sins here are jealousy, envy, idolatry, and selfish ambition. Wanting what does not belong to you and thinking that it should sets the stage for manipulation. It justifies making yourself happy at the expense of others, and results in hatred, discord, dissensions, factions, and fits of rage. Manipulation intimidates and divides to conquer. God is not pleased with any of these attitudes, and He deals very harshly with those who insist on displaying this type of behavior. Though it may work for a season, the final result is never pleasant. Jezebel got her way, but in the end she paid with the life of her husband, herself, and her generations of children who followed. They all died ugly deaths, proving that your personal realm of control will not outlast your soul. "He who leads the upright along an evil path will fall into his own trap, but the blameless will receive a good inheritance" (Proverbs 28:10 NIV).

Taking Advantage of His Weakness

Some of you are thinking to yourself that you don't know any women who are that evil. You don't know any women who have a bevy of male lackeys following them around, jumping at their beck and call, who weave treachery as easily as they stir a bowl of soup. You're right—some are a little more subtle with their stuff. Delilah, known in some sermons as "De-lie-yah," was real smooth at working her game. Her specialty was seduction—using her eyes, her lips, her hands, her body, and her perfume. It was a total woman thing. She drugged Samson with her femininity, slowly squeezing the life out of him by extracting the secret of his strength. This is a classic example of using a man's secrets against him to further yourself. Delilah lived in the valley of Sorek. The word "Sorek" means "choice vines." Vines attached to a building look harmless enough, even pretty. But left unchecked, they can destroy the entire structure. They can actually creep through its cement and devastate the walls with huge cracks and holes. They can cover windows, shutting out all light from the outside world. Before you know it, the whole building has been claimed by what appeared to be a harmless vine. In translation, a man is rendered senseless once you've worked your way between the cracks of his armor. When he's lost his discernment and can't see, he's wide open for all of his defenses to crumble to dust. He is then a sitting target for destruction.

Delilah knew all of this as she prepared her house with incense and prepared herself with costly toiletries and seductive clothing. She carefully planned her time with Samson as she prepared his favorite dishes and selected just the right wine for dulling his senses. She was a master at mixing the perfect amount of womanly expertise with the ideal proportion of childlike naïveté. She knew the combination could be lethal when used just right. So she fed him, stroked him, and set him up for the kill. With visions of the silver that had been promised to her for delivering Samson's secret to the Philistines, she set to work. She poured on the flattery, appealing to his ego, telling him how much his strength impressed her. You can just imagine what else she said, right? And while he lay basking in her praise, well-fed, well-loved, and well-appreciated, she queried him as to the source of his 'awesome strength. Knowing he shouldn't reveal it, he humored her with a lie—a lie she delivered to the Philistines, who found out in a most unpleasant way that the information was false. With this, Delilah stepped up her program. She had pretended to be a good sport during the first go-round, but when her plan failed a second time, she pulled out her last secret weapon—whining, subtle at first, then building in insistence until it exploded in a classic accusation: "You don't love me! If you did, you would..." You know the routine. Like a dripping faucet, she wore him down, and then, appealing to the heart of the rescuer within him, she finally got her wish. And while he lay sleeping in her lap, she called another man to come cut his hair off, thus ushering him to his death.

Delilah won her man's trust, wooing him to a place of complete rest with her and then making him the victim of other men by exposing his secrets. Well, as you know, Samson's hair eventually grew back, he leveled the Philistine temple with one push, and then he died amidst the rubble. What happened to Delilah? God only knows. Perhaps she, too, died at the temple, taking one last look at her handiwork. I wouldn't be surprised. Truly, there is a pattern that emerges here. Women who manipulate might get what they want momentarily, but it costs them more than they gain. In the process, they lose the men in their lives and they also lose themselves. God has a much more rewarding design for the power of influence that He has bestowed upon us.

Esther actually used the same recipe as Delilah, minus the deception, whining, and accusations. She prepared herself to be pleasing in appearance to her husband. She, too, fed him and stroked his ego by making him feel that his company was reward enough for her. Though she wanted something, she made sure that her husband first was fully satisfied before she sought her own desire. She waited until he asked her for her request, and then she very simply stated her need, leaving the final judgment to him. How could she be so calm in the

---

This is where true femininity emerges as a clear victor. It triumphs over the barriers of misunderstanding. It disarms the hard of heart. It gently leads to a better way. It repairs the breach between those who have and those who are wanting.

---

face of such life-threatening circumstances? What would keep her from trying to manipulate the situation in the face of such a dire emergency? First of all, she felt that her desire was God's desire. She was confident that God would have the final say if she stayed in the right position. She had made her first appeal to God. If God did not speak to the king's heart, then obviously He had another plan for her and her people. Remember, she said, "If I perish, I perish." She knew that her life hung in the balance of an even greater authority than her husband. As she explained her reason for alarm, she knew that her fate really did not lie in man's hands. This freed her to move with serene calm should the king choose not to intervene on her behalf. Ultimately, it would be God's will that would be done. And how could a man with any kind of a heart resist such a countenance? This is where true femininity emerges as a clear victor. It triumphs over the barriers of misunderstanding. It disarms the hard of heart. It gently leads to a better way. It repairs the breach between those who have and those who are wanting.

In the book of 1 Samuel, Abigail did not exactly have time on her side, but she utilized the time that she had well, presenting David with food and provisions to abate his anger. She then appealed to his sense of judgment on behalf of God's purposes, and this kept him from making a decision he would have regretted later. It stopped David from moving forward with his plan to destroy her household because of the stupidity of her husband. Abigail made sure that David was well-fed. Have you noticed that food seems to pop up in all of these stories? Perhaps it's because a woman really does feed the soul of a man. What she feeds him can either strengthen him to do the right thing, or poison him to render him susceptible to making foolish choices. So be careful what you stir up in that man! The next thing Abigail did was to give David credit for having good sense. This is important. David was now freed to think clearly and to make a sound decision without feeling like he was rolling over. Far too many times it is not *what* a woman says to a man, it is the *way* she says it that causes him to rebel against perfectly good advice.

"Perfume and incense bring joy to the heart, and the pleasantness of ones friend springs from his earnest counsel" (Proverbs 27:9 NIV).

"An honest answer is like a kiss on the lips" (Proverbs 24:26 NIV).

"Reckless words pierce like a sword, but the tongue of the wise brings healing. Truthful lips endure forever, but a lying tongue lasts only a moment" (Proverbs 12:18,19 NIV).

"Pleasant words are a honeycomb, sweet to the soul and healing to the bones" (Proverbs 16:24 NIV).

"A [woman] of knowledge uses words with restraint" (Proverbs 17:27 NIV).

Why do you think that Pilate, in the heat of making a decision concerning the sentencing of Jesus, stopped to consider his wife's opinion on the matter? Here he sat, surrounded by people screaming their heads off in the heat of the day. Tension was at fever pitch, and in the middle of all this turmoil everything stops. One little note from his wife, warning Pilate not to be involved in determining what happened to Jesus, that she'd had a dream about this man which troubled her deeply, was enough to make him wash his hands of sealing Jesus' fate. Pilate's wife must have had a reputation for giving him sound counsel. He knew that she watched over his soul and covered his heart. Pilate also knew that his wife's counsel was based on her watching out for his best interest. Hers was pure counsel that he could trust. This is the heart of a feminine and virtuous woman.

"A wife of noble character who can find? She is worth far more than rubies. Her husband has full confidence in her and lacks nothing of value. She brings him good, not harm, all the days of her life" (Proverbs 31:10-12 NIV).

The virtuous woman set her man's mind at ease, thus preparing him to deal effectively with his world. She *influenced* him to make decisions that would not only ensure victory in his daily life, but would also keep him on the path to completing his God-ordained purpose. My favorite song as a child was the one from *Mary Poppins* that went, "Just a spoonful of sugar helps the medicine go down." It is true!

A fable comes to mind here, one involving a little bet between the North Wind and the Sun. One day, as both observed a man walking down a lonesome road, they wagered as to which one of the two could get the man to remove his topcoat. The North Wind, full of confidence, decided to go first. He filled his cheeks with Arctic air and blew with all his might. The man, feeling the chill, merely pulled his coat tighter about him. So the North Wind blew some more, only to have the man pull his coat even tighter with each frigid gust of the wind's breath. Completely exhausted, the North Wind finally stepped aside to allow the Sun to take a try. Well, the Sun just mounted up high above the clouds and began to shine his warmest rays. He quietly shone with all the effervescence he could muster. After a while, the man began to grow warm, so he loosened the folds of his coat. And still the Sun did not move; he simply continued to shine in his warm, quiet way. After a while the man began to perspire, the Sun's warmth cheering his chilled bones. Wiping his brow, he looked toward the Sun with a welcoming smile and removed his coat. Force versus warmth, a little patience, and a generous dose of giving—you figure it out.

Becoming One

It is important to note that having a profound effect on the men in our world brings us full circle back to the issue of submission.

> "Wives, in the same way be submissive to your husbands so that, if any of them do not believe the word, they may be won over without words by the behavior of their wives, when they see the purity and reverence of your lives" (1 Peter 3:1,2 NIV).

God has given us the incredible power to convert men! Only a submitted woman can influence a man, or any type of authority, for that matter. The goal is willing cooperation. Going along begrudgingly does not build loyalty, but submission lowers the resistance to sound instruction and paves the way for a profitable exchange between the two parties involved. In the arena of marriage, where becoming one is God's mandate, submission is essential to achieving this goal. And this brings me to an area I would like to carefully address for your consideration. I have watched with increasing alarm the tendency for a woman not to take her husband's name when she marries. Or she chooses to hyphenate her name and her husband's name. I have to ask: What is your motive? If it's a matter of your individualism, then you open the door to the serpent causing problems in your marriage. Think about it. On one hand, he has women feeling that they are incomplete without a man and that they must have a man's name to take away their reproach. Then, when they finally get a man, the serpent tells them that they need to maintain their own identity. The serpent hates marriage, and if he can't keep women bound up single, he will wreak havoc on their marriages any way he can. As insignificant as this whole name business may seem, can it be that it is actually the symptom of an even deeper problem? I believe that a woman's refusal to take her husband's name serves a mandate against her marriage. It sets her up for a hard time, or even failure, based on a divided beginning.

Remember, names are very significant to God. Names mean something. Is your stating that you must keep your own name for business purposes a roundabout way of saying that what was going on in your world before you met your husband is more important to you? Or that you don't trust this man enough to disregard previous experiences? You better believe the serpent will drop that seed in his spirit and water it big-time! This sets your husband up to become vulnerable to someone who appears to be more submissive than you. It also confuses your children. Even though he, in his attempt to seem like a liberated '90s kind of man, murmurs that whatever you want to do is fine with him, it is still an insult to his spirit. If it's not, you had better wonder why not. Perhaps he thinks the deal he's getting is a good compromise for selling out his cover over you. If he'll abdicate in the name department, chances are he'll abdicate in other areas of your marriage. He won't step up to cover you in many ways. But a man who is grounded spiritually, knowing his place and what God has ordered him to be to you, will take your denial of his name as a personal affront. It fights against the order of the universe, God's divine law, which decrees that a man shall leave his mother and father, cleave to his wife, and the *two* shall become *one*. All of this gets lost in the shuffle as we opt for appearing contemporary, sophisticated, and informed, but at what cost?

> "Who is wise and understanding among you? Let him show it by his good life, by deeds done in the humility that comes from wisdom. But if you harbor bitter envy and selfish ambition in your hearts, do not boast about it or deny the truth. Such 'wisdom' does not come down from heaven but is earthly, unspiritual, of the devil. For where you have envy and selfish ambition, there you find disorder and every evil practice" (James 3:13-16 NIV).

So it seems that what is politically correct isn't necessarily spiritually correct. Wisdom and humility combined are God's definition of a power couple. I remember that a friend of mine who went on to become incredibly wealthy was extremely unassuming and quiet. Whenever I messed with him about how quiet he was, he would always respond that you grow wiser by being quiet. He was always drinking in information. He never felt the need to share how much he knew, but it showed up on the bottom line of his life.

When we as women envy a man's position of leadership and entertain the selfish ambition of running everything the way we want it to go, the end result is disorder in the household. And that will leave the door wide open for every evil practice to enter. For those of you who indulge yourselves in this business of him going to his church and you going to yours, all I can say is that you are a brave woman. There are not enough men in church as it is, and you allow your man to go to church unprotected? That is throwing him to the wolves. Never overestimate who you are to your husband, and never underestimate the damage the serpent can do when you're not looking. Remember, the family who prays together, stays together.

If you are married, your goal is to become one with your husband—one in the spirit, one in your passions, one in name. Why? Because marriage is a covenant. A covenant is based on death. *Somebody* has to die in order for a covenant to be fulfilled. Actually, *both people* have to die. When God made a covenant with Abraham, He took one animal, split it down the middle, and then passed between the two halves to seal His promise of faithfulness to Abraham. That's what God wants to do with you and your husband. He wants both of you to come together, render yourselves dead, and let Him pass through. It is God in the center of your marriage that fuses you into a reflection of the oneness He shares with His Son and with the Holy Ghost. Though they are three separate parts, they are one. They counsel amongst themselves. They agree in all things. None moves apart from the other, yet each is considered equally powerful because they feed off of one another. This is the intimacy God felt Adam was lacking when He said, "It is not good for man to be alone." This is what God created in the garden. He first took one man, then took a woman out of the man, and finally put them back together—kind of like twins.

We've all heard stories of how twins living apart from each other have amazingly felt exactly what the other twin was going through. That's the way God wants a husband and wife to be—practically living inside of one another. Have you ever noticed that when you see an old couple who have been together forever, they even begin to look alike? They can finish one another's sentences. They seem so settled and happy. Individual agendas are a thing of the past. All the fight is gone. They've settled into one another. That's becoming one. I think Shakespeare said it best: "Love is not love which alters when it alteration finds." In other words, love automatically is going to change some things, and you won't even mind.

> "Two are better than one, because they have a good return for their work. If one falls down, his friend can help him up, But pity the man who falls and has no one to help him up! Also, if two lie down together, they will keep warm. But how can one keep warm alone? Though one may be overpowered, two can defend themselves. A cord of three strands is not quickly broken" (Ecclesiastes 4:9-12 NIV).

There are benefits to this partnership thing. There is a giving that comes from love that goes the extra mile. The cost never matters to true love. We know that God so loved us that He gave the life of His very own Son. Because God was seeking a covenant relationship with us, death was involved. Now, that's some love. Do I hear any other volunteers? Love is selfless. Love is humbling because it causes you to cast all caution to the wind, to give and give again. Now, that's if you're *truly* in love. So here's my humble suggestion: Crown that man by taking his name. It is his cover over you. Don't deny him that. You really don't have an identity to protect, anyway. Your life is supposed to be hidden in Christ.

> "I am crucified with Christ: nevertheless I live; yet not I, but Christ liveth in me: and the life which I now live in the flesh I live by the faith of the Son of God, who loved me, and gave himself for me" (Galatians 2:20 KJV).

Remember, when God created woman out of man, He saw them as one from the beginning. For Him there was no separation in identity. Though the two had different functions, they made up the whole of one another. He called them both man. So keep in mind that every time you see the word "man" in the Bible, that includes *you* because you were taken from man. God speaks to us universally, unless it is a specific gender reference of some sort, such as men should not wear clothes pertaining to a woman. In light of this information, know that your oneness is on a higher order than what the world purports. As you and your mate strive to look like Christ, submitting to God as you submit to one another, you will end up looking alike. Make submitting to the personification of love your aim, and oneness will be achieved. As you work toward oneness with your mate, giving him room to be who God has called him to be in your world, you will find that submission will be mutual. You will be freed to be the voice of influence who God designed you to be, doing your man good and not evil all of his days. He, in return, will be freed to respond to the jewels you deposit in his spirit and become an even greater blessing to you. And that, my friend, is the grand prize.

> "When God created man, he made him in the likeness of God. He created them male and female and blessed them. And when they were created, he called them 'man'" (Genesis 5:1,2 NIV).

Dear Heavenly Father, thank You for the extraordinarily powerful gift You've given me—the gift of influence. Teach me to wield it well. Make me mindful of Your Word as I exercise my gift. Keep me in remembrance of Your purposes in my life, as well as those whom You put within my sphere of influence. Help me never to abuse the hearts and wills of others. Let me know when I have crossed the line to manipulation. Lead me by Your Spirit, that I might know when to plant and when to let go in order for You to water and bear the increase in the lives of those around me. As I yield myself to Your leadership, help me to yield to those whom You have placed over me. Help me to do it joyfully. Open my eyes to see the reward of submission. And Lord, with those who make it difficult to follow Your design, move in a special way and give me a testimony of victory. In Jesus' name. Amen.

NINE

Going over His Head

She watched the glass
        now empty
    badly in need of a refill
        her arms hung heavily by her sides
            too weary from her constant revisiting
                of a task she longed for him to do
                he too waited
                    accustomed to her frequent attendance
                        he saw no need to break a familiar pattern
                    though he knew it was his duty
                        to refresh her
                        to fill her
    she had done so well
        refreshing herself
            he now had no memory
                of how to go about the task
    and he wondered why her eyes were so angry
            though her speech did not give her away
    the distance he felt from her body
        when he reached to caress her
            left unanswered questions in his mind
                that he dared not utter
                    afraid of the responsibility
                        her answer might require on his part
            and so he waited
                waited for her to refill the glass
        but instead she just stood there
                with her arms dangling like leaden appendages
            looking up toward the heavens
    lips moving silently
        pouring out her soul
    tears streaming down

until they overflowed the brim of the glass
and as she reached for it
the unthinkable occurred
the glass tipped over
spilling its contents
rolling
rolling
rolling out of her reach
landing at his feet
and she still standing
not moving except
to see if her prayers had been answered
watched him bend to pick it up
staring
as if at a foreign object
finally a glint of recognition lighting his face
he revisited his initial call
filling it with himself
he gave her to drink
and she partook of his offering gratefully
still looking toward heaven
and then into his eyes
now filling with understanding
as the anger left hers
making room for softness in her gaze
as her arms regained their strength
no longer exhausted from carrying
both their loads
with one arm unfettered
she was now free
to embrace him
truly her glass was full...

*G*ive me children or else I die!" Rachel bitterly flung her words at Jacob, glaring at him as if he were the worst kind of traitor. How dare he give another woman children when it was with her that his heart took its solace? What type of cruel joke was this? She, his beloved, was barren while her sister Leah, who had gained Jacob as a husband through deception, gave him children as easily as she sneezed. What had she done to deserve this most humiliating station? She wanted her husband to fix this mess and fix it now! But all he could do was look at her as if she had gone mad. This was far beyond his control. They were both at the mercy of One higher than themselves.

Sometimes our own insecurities can cause us to demand things from men that are not humanly possible for them to give. We wonder what type of evil hand God has dealt us when the man in our life doesn't seem to assist us in being fruitful, be it pregnancy, financial assistance, or just plain ole simple happiness. Women so often wonder why, after clinching the dream of gaining a spouse, they still feel empty and unfulfilled. Perhaps this is the most painful lesson that any human being can learn. There is a place in our hearts that only God can fill. To rely on anyone else to deliver joy and fulfillment to our door is to come up sadly wanting, peering around the doorframe of our lives to see if the deliveryman forgot to leave the package.

It is important for us to understand the revelation that fruitfulness comes from the Lord, not from man. God's command to Adam and Eve in the garden was to be fruitful and multiply. Webster defines being fruitful as being abundantly productive. Adam and Eve's individual call was to bear fruit, as in the fruit of the spirit, as well as natural productivity. Their mutual call was to multiply—multiply others who bore fruit. God would meet them in the process and add to what they produced. Fruitfulness is where our true contentment lies, and this is made possible by the handiwork of God Himself.

> "I will look on you with favor and make you fruitful and increase your numbers, and I will keep my covenant with you" (Leviticus 26:9 NIV).

> "Whoever has will be given more, and he will have an abundance. Whoever does not have, even what he has will be taken from him" (Matthew 13:12 NIV).

Remember what happened when Jesus spotted the fig tree that bore no fruit? He cursed it. As far as he was concerned, it was already dead. To not bear fruit is to be dead. We cannot blame anyone but ourselves for our lives being barren of fruit. God has commanded us to be fruitful. He has equipped us to be fruitful, whether single or married. No human being should affect your fruitfulness, unless they are adding to it by provoking you to greater good works. If they are subtracting from you, causing your fruit to wither or grow bitter, you should reconsider why you associate with that person.

Single women must understand that they are as close to their mate as they're ever going to be right where they are

At the end of the day, your relationship with your mate is only as good as your relationship with God.

now. Married women, come along with me on this one; it also applies to you. A single friend of mine shared this with me one day over dinner. She had been asking God where her mate was, and He kept answering, "I've got your mate right here." To which she would reply, "Right here *where?*" Finally God opened her understanding to see that her mate was inside of Him. How could this be? Simple. God knows where your mate is right now. He knows everything there is to know about your mate. Even if you met him today, you would still have to go to God to find out things about him. Married women, when your husband isn't talking, God can supply the information he is leaving out. At the end of the day, your relationship with your mate is only as good as your relationship with God. He is the bridge between the two of our lives.

But I'm getting ahead of myself. I want to look at what happens with men in our lives on two levels—when we expect the impossible from them, and when they fail to step up to the plate and take their God-assigned position in our lives.

Now, Rachel had a problem. She wanted to have children, but she was barren. Her sister Leah, also married to her husband, was having children every time Jacob looked at her, or so it seemed in Rachel's eyes. So passionate was this plea on her heart that she exploded, swearing to Jacob that she would die if he didn't give her a child. Jacob asked her an interesting question: "Am I in the place of God...?" (Genesis 30:2). Is that man, or the desire for a man in your life, in the place of God? Are you making demands he can do nothing about? Is there a void in you that is robbing you of the happiness that could be yours regardless of your circumstance?

I always suspect that Rachel's relationship with God was not a close one based on the fact that when she and her husband finally left her father's house, she took some of her father's gods with her. They must have been majorly important ones because Laban pursued them in order to reclaim them. Jacob was insulted, as he felt that everyone should have known by now that he did not worship the same gods they did. In fact, he felt so strongly that no one amongst them had taken the gods that he declared death to the person who had taken them, not knowing that his own beloved wife was guilty of the deed. Rachel hid them under her camel's saddle and sat on it as they searched through all of the camp's belongings. Claiming she was weak from her time of the month, she prevented them from checking beneath the saddle, and the men left without finding them. So Rachel unknowingly set herself up to be cursed by her own husband. As a matter of fact, the irony goes even deeper. She said that she would die if she didn't have a child, right? Well, she died in childbirth with her second son. Sometimes the thing you think you can't live without is the same thing that will kill you.

Someone once sent me a fable called, "Things Aren't Always What They Seem." It told the story of two angels who visited the house of some wealthy people. The people were very unkind to the angels and, though they could have offered them better accommodations, forced them to sleep on the basement floor. During the night, one of the angels got up and repaired a hole that had been in the basement wall. The next day they moved on, stopping for the night this time at the home of some very poor people whose sole possession was a cow that provided milk for their meager income. The poor couple was very kind to the angels, even giving up their bed so that the two visitors could get a comfortable sleep. The next morning they awoke to find that the couple's cow had died. Well, the younger angel became very upset with the older angel. He wanted to know why the older angel had allowed this dreadful thing to happen, especially in light of the fact that he had been good enough to repair the wall at the mean people's home. Why couldn't he have protected these nice people from disaster? The older angel replied that he shouldn't be upset if he didn't have all the facts. He then went on to explain that he had only repaired the hole in the wall because the mean people were greedy and he didn't want them to find the gold that he knew was hidden there. In the middle of the night, the death angel had visited the poor couple to take the wife, and the older angel had negotiated for him to take the cow instead. The moral is, you need to think twice before you draw a conclusion. What you see isn't always what you get, and sometimes it's better that way. I always say, God's prevention is God's protection. But when we are in the thick of the wanting, we can't see the wisdom in any form of denial.

After so much weeping on Rachel's part, it still wasn't Jacob's efforts that got Rachel pregnant. The Bible says that "*God* remembered Rachel; He listened to her and opened her womb" (Genesis 30:23 NIV, emphasis added). It was *God*, not her husband. Even after God showed up on Rachel's behalf, she clung to other gods. These false gods brought a curse upon her life, and she died while delivering her second child.

Standing in Need

Now, Hannah was a woman who knew her God. She knew that her barren womb was not something her husband could do anything about, so she went straight to the source. She poured out her soul to God. God heard her and opened her womb. She then gave that child up to God. After that, God honored Hannah's sacrifice and gave her several more children. That sounds simple enough, but it doesn't mean that Hannah didn't go through anything. She, also, was married to a man with an additional wife who seemed to have no trouble having children. To make matters worse, this other wife provoked Hannah out of jealousy and sought to irritate her by teasing her about the fact that she was childless. Poor Hannah would get so upset that she would weep and couldn't eat. Couldn't eat! I'm sorry, but nothing stops *me* from eating. This woman, though, couldn't eat, and here her husband was truly in love with her, so much so that he gave her a double portion when they went to sacrifice before the Lord. This was why Peninnah, the other wife, was picking at Hannah in the first place. Though she had children, she knew she was playing second fiddle, and she wasn't about to allow Hannah to enjoy her most-loved position in peace. Now, Hannah's insightful husband, Elkanah, asked Hannah a very interesting question here. He said, "Don't I mean more to you than ten sons?"

That is deep! Hannah had a classic case of "One-Tree-Itis," a disease that hits us all. It causes us to overlook all the other trees from which we can eat of freely and instead long after the one tree we can't have. Our desire for that *one thing* will cause us to stop eating. We will stop eating life and all that it offers. "One-Tree-Itis" paralyzes us. It shuts us down. We cease to sample all our other options. Hannah was not free to enjoy the gift that her husband truly loved her and would do anything to make her happy because she got stuck on her barrenness. Keep in mind here that she had some help concentrating on this blaring fact. Many of us would probably be alright if there weren't some friend or relative around to constantly rub salt in the wounds of our desires. But when they speak, pointing out our lack, the heat is on. The pressure is almost suffocating, and we feel we have to produce something just to silence the voices. And God says to us all, "Don't I mean more to you than ten of those? Don't you crave My purposes being fulfilled in your life more than that temporal thing that you so badly long for?" What's your answer?

When Hannah had had enough of everyone and their opinions, she got serious with God. She got so serious that she was praying and no sound was coming out. Have you ever prayed until you were speechless? Well, Hannah did. And God heard her. Not only did He hear her, He had Eli, the high priest, tell her that her request had been granted. And because Hannah's confidence was in God, not in her husband, she went her way with a smile on her face. As a matter of fact, the first thing she did after that was to eat something. When you get a word from God concerning the things that lay heavy on your heart, you'll get freed up to partake of all He has put before you to enjoy in the meantime. Nothing affects a man like a woman with a downcast countenance. He never knows what to do with the information that you are sad, especially if it is a situation he can do nothing about. He will retreat out of his own sense of failure. So get a word from the Lord in order to restore the joy level in your surroundings. Hannah ate something, and her countenance wasn't downcast anymore. She went and worshiped the Lord because she had a promise with which she could run. She went back home, lay with her husband, and conceived.

This applies to any of us who expect the man in our world to produce peace, self-worth, validation, or even material things. God is ultimately our source of all these treasures. We will strive, weep, and deprive ourselves of opportunities to live a full life if we put our hope in a person to fulfill our expectations. Trust me, it won't happen. There's only One who delivers everything our hearts crave.

"The LORD is my shepherd, I shall not be in want" (Psalm 23:1 NIV).

"Woe to them that go down to Egypt for help; and stay on horses, and trust in chariots, because they are many; and in horsemen, because they are very strong; but they look not unto the Holy One of Israel, neither seek the LORD!" (Isaiah 31:1 KJV).

When our sights get set on the arm of flesh, we will always be let down. Man can only do so much, but God can do any and every thing. It is not a man who will make our life fruitful, but rather our own yielding to God's call to fulfill our purpose through the use of our gifts and talents. As we live in the moment, making the best of every occasion to lift the spirits of those around us, our world will change for the better. We will become more joyful and productive individuals who now attract a different type of person into our inner circle. It is of the utmost importance that we as women become complete, whole individuals as Christ completes the vacuum within us. Only then will we attract whole men who can step up to the plate in their relationship to us. Why? Because we won't settle for anything less.

Well, Michelle, you say, I'm already stuck with a man who has just abdicated on me. How do I get him to step up to the plate and just do what God would have him to do? You know, the basics—like being a for-real husband and a father? Not an absentee bill-payer. I know some of you are thinking, hmm...him paying the bills? Now, wouldn't that be refreshing! Yeah, girl, how *do* I maintain my femininity when my man won't help me? How do I keep my dress on while he's trying to squeeze me into wearing the pants in the family? The answer is easier to say than it is to do. Stop rescuing him.

B-b-bbut, Michelle! If I don't pay the bills, the lights will get cut off! If I don't do this or that, it won't get done! I understand all of that *but* do you understand that until you create a void for him to fill, he will not rise to the occasion? In some cases, your rescue attempts have circumvented lessons the Lord wanted to teach that man. When Jacob wrestled with the angel of the Lord, he wrestled alone. He had already sent his wives and children ahead of him. Though they were a part of his life and their destiny was wrapped up in whatever happened to him, whether he went backward or forward on the journey was between him and God. I could just see it now if the wives were still with Jacob when the wrestling match began. They all would have been involved, trying to pull the stranger off of Jacob. Stop, you're going to hurt him! Well, sometimes a man needs to acquire a limp to find out what time it is. Then he'll find that it is time to rise up and become the man God has called him to be.

> "Husbands, love your wives, even as Christ also loved the church, and gave himself for it" (Ephesians 5:25 KJV).

> "So ought men to love their wives as their own bodies. He that loveth his wife loveth himself" (Ephesians 5:28 KJV).

> "Likewise, ye husbands, dwell with them according to knowledge, giving honour unto the wife, as unto the weaker vessel, and as being heirs together of the grace of life; that your prayers be not hindered" (1 Peter 3:7 KJV).

Yes, God really did mean for that man to take good care of you. But he'll only do that if you let him. One of my male friends put me in check the other day. We were walking along and I was telling him about this very book. So he said to me, "Well then, if you're supposed to be so feminine, why are you lugging around those two heavy bags? You didn't even ask me to carry them for you!" I laughed and promptly handed them over. To be perfectly honest, I wasn't even thinking about it. I'm so used to carrying my own load that I simply forget. But I got the hang of it really fast. As we got ready to leave the building to go to his car, which was parked a short distance away, I looked outside and saw the snow. Casting a glance his way as he relayed to me that the car wasn't far, I said, "Well, if you were truly doing your job, and I were truly being a feminine woman, you would go get the car and come back to pick me up." He stopped short and said, "Oh, okay! You wait right here; I'll be happy to do that!" I chuckled to myself as he went his way and returned minutes later with a big grin on his face. He was quite pleased with himself that he was being such a gentleman, and I made some quip like, "My hero," or something along those lines. Needless to say, I've never had to ask him to go get the car again. It's automatic.

Now, that's a simplistic story compared to the major issues some of you are dealing with, but the same principle applies. First, you must begin with yourself. Just because he has abdicated his responsibilities as a man does not mean that you roll over and resign yourself to the fact that he just doesn't seem to get it. No! Keep your expectations intact, and let him know that you expect him to be the man he's supposed to be. Follow that through by leaving the space for whatever he is supposed to be doing vacant. That means if he doesn't do it, it doesn't get done. A pastor friend of mine told about a lady parishioner who complained about her husband not paying the bills on time. My friend told her to allow the lights to be cut off. Well, this piece of advice just rocked this lady's world. How could she do that? Simple, replied the pastor, don't rescue him from his own negligence. When the lights go off, he will become acutely aware of his responsibilities and do something about it. After that, it won't happen again.

I know this is true based on two conversations I have had with male friends who were discussing the pros and cons of leaving their wives. In both cases, the reason the man remained was because he didn't think his wife could function without him. Though these men felt that they were no longer in love with their wives, they were of the opinion that their wives were still wonderful women and they felt responsible for their well-being. Each man couldn't bear the thought of a woman who did not deserve to be hurt having her world crumble all around her because her husband wasn't there to keep up the walls. So they went back home and applied themselves to making their marriages work.

Sarah did not rescue Abraham, I can tell you that. When he twice passed her off as his sister in foreign territory and she was taken, she didn't open her mouth. After God intervened in both cases, the kings asked for an explanation from *Abraham. He* was held accountable. They didn't address Sarah at all, never asked her why she didn't say something. Abraham was her covering. He was responsible.

This is why God asked Adam where he was after the fall in the garden. God knew that Eve had taken the first bite, yet he addressed Adam. In God's design, Adam was responsible for Eve, and he had slipped on the job. He had relinquished his role as protector. Because he did not intervene in Eve's deception and then—even worse—willfully rebelled by joining her in her sin, he would be punished. Because Adam wanted to do things his way and not God's way, he would now find out how difficult it would be to do what was once simple with God, without Him.

It was simple to lead the woman when Adam did it with God. Now, leading her without God only resulted in her rebellion. The woman would rebel, the ground would rebel, everything in his world would rebel against him. But he would still have to produce because it was demanded of him. So just imagine what would happen if the demand were taken away. You got it! Man would sit down for a long rest, relieved the struggle was over. Now is the time to remind that man he has been redeemed from the curse of the law. It's time to pick up his cross and, while he's at it, he can take the garbage out. He can take time with his children and be a good example to them. He can cover you and protect you from the things that threaten to stretch you beyond your personal resources. He can treat you the way he treats his own body, as he has been commanded by the Lord, which means he will take good care of you.

The Hearts of the Fathers

Adam also abdicated as a parent. Where was he when Cain killed Abel? I know he didn't fix his lips to blame that one on Eve. Where were the fathering skills to teach his sons how to make the right kind of sacrifice to the Lord? Cain was probably the one who worked closest with Adam because he worked the soil as Adam had. Because struggling with the soil was part of the curse for Adam, we know that this was his vocation after leaving the garden. So Adam taught Cain how to work the soil, but he overlooked the most important area of instruction in his son's life—how to walk with God, how to surrender to God by delivering the right sacrifice, his first fruits. So who was the influence teaching Abel the right sacrifice? Because he tended flocks, that meant Abel spent a lot of time away and alone. Perhaps in his time of solitude he came to a place of intimacy with God on his own. We can't honestly say, but Cain killed Abel because God accepted Abel's sacrifice but was not pleased with Cain's. And the only One who rebuked him was God. Interesting, isn't it? Perhaps Adam did not realize the full extent of damage his lack of parenting would reap. But he got it straight on the next round. Eve gave birth to Seth after this, and he was a godly man who began to plant a godly lineage in the earth. After the declaration of Seth's birth, men began to call on the name of the Lord. The death of Abel was sobering for everyone.

Especially when it comes to your children, it is important that you allow your man room to step up to the plate. Make your needs known to him and then step back. King David abdicated as a father, and look at the mess that followed. We never hear of a wife telling David he needed to deal with the situation that was brewing amongst his children. David's son Amnon raped his stepsister Tamar. Tamar was the sister of Absalom, another of David's sons. The way the story goes, word of the situation got back to David. While he was very angry, he didn't do anything about it. Meanwhile, here was his daughter completely broken and disgraced, and his son furious because his father took no action. This led Absalom to conclude that if his father wouldn't do anything about it, he would mete out his own punishment as he saw fit for the crime. So Absalom killed his brother in cold blood at a banquet. Oh, but the family turmoil doesn't stop there! This same son, Absalom, was now bitter against his father David. Driven by this same spirit of revenge, he proceeded to lead a revolt against the kingdom. I'm sure in his mind he was thinking, if my dad can't even rule his own house, why should he get to rule a nation? And in the process, because Absalom concluded that David didn't think of rape as a crime that should be dealt with, he helped himself to a couple of his father's concubines, in full view of the public. So there!

When fathers refuse to fill their "daddy shoes," chaos is inevitable. Children become embittered; they know when parents aren't doing what they're supposed to be doing. Their response is to do what Absalom did, which was round up his own group of malcontents who were just as angry and rebellious as he was and begin to stage a revolt. This was the original gang. It affected the entire household. Because David wouldn't step up to the parenting plate, he was forced to vacate the premises, period. Because God takes no pleasure in rebellion and because His relationship with David was such a close one regardless of his failings, He restored the kingdom back to David—but not without a serious loss. As Absalom made his getaway, his hair, which was his pride and joy, got caught in a tree and Joab, David's general, killed him. The pain that David felt was excruciating because he realized it was his own lack of fatherhood that had brought about his son's dreadful end. He wished he could exchange the life he never gave when his son was alive in exchange for his tragic death.

But Bathsheba wouldn't have any of it when it came to her son Solomon. She made sure that David had an active part in the child rearing. She kept him cognizant of the fact that he was grooming Israel's next king, that a man's touch was needed in the life of a young boy coming of age. With her gentle nudging and reminders, David excelled where he had failed so miserably before. Bathsheba spoke up without demanding, and then left room for David to do what needed to be done.

Because a man craves respect and praise so much, he will rise to the occasion when he knows he is being counted on. "I need" are good words to use with men because they have planted in their spirits a God-given drive to fix things and to restore order. If a man feels like you've got it covered, he will allow you to take the whole ball and run with it. Therefore, it is important for you to step back and let a man rise or fall on his own. This is where the muscles of character are built. Here's a scientific fact for you to ponder. If you help a butterfly out of its cocoon, it will die. In the actual struggle to get out of the cocoon, blood rushes to all of the butterfly's veins, and this empowers its wings to fly. Without the struggle, the wings never unfold properly or gain the strength they need. Therefore, the butterfly is hindered from flight and dies. The same thing applies to men and women. We just don't like to watch the struggle. It looks too painful, especially when you see your loved one heading straight for a fall. There is something innate in a woman that makes her want to stick out her hand and break the fall. Don't do it! You might interrupt his fall and break your arm in the process.

Remember the story I told earlier about things not always being what they seem? Well, that lesson also applies in this situation. Sometimes a failure—a fall—is the best thing that can happen to any of us when we get offtrack. It stops us from continuing in the wrong direction. Some parts of Scripture make the apostle Paul sound very harsh and unsympathetic, and yet when you closely examine what he was saying, you realize he understood this very point from his own experience. Sometimes people have to come to the end of themselves in order to have a true revelation on where exactly they are supposed to be. In one portion of Scripture, Paul mentions a situation about a man in sin whom everyone around him is trying to handle in delicate fashion. You know, not being judgmental, not rocking the boat, and all that sort of thing. Rather, it was the talk of the congregation. But Paul saw the bigger picture. He knew that if the man was coddled in his sinful state, he would never get right and that ultimately his behavior would begin to rub off on others in the congregation.

> "Shouldn't you rather have been filled with grief and have put out of your fellowship the man who did this?...When you are assembled in the name of our Lord Jesus and I am with you in spirit, and the power of our Lord Jesus is present, hand this man over to Satan, so that the sinful nature may be destroyed and his spirit saved on the day of the Lord" (1 Corinthians 5:2,4,5 NIV).

That's pretty heavy, you say, but think about it this way. When a man does not do what he has been designed to do, he is in sin. His sin affects his entire household. If you are an enabler, you're back in the garden with the serpent, receiving fresh judgment all over again. Christ came to redeem us from this scene. We do not have to enlist in a sequel. Turning him over to Satan sounds strong, but what Paul was really suggesting was that this man be allowed to experience the full consequences of his actions in order to come to his senses. Don't gloss over it. Call it what it is. Don't dress it up and call it by another name because he's sweet and he just lays down on the job in this one area. No, God holds him accountable as He held Adam accountable to fulfill his entire call as a man. As a man's wife, you are called to assist him in the fulfillment of his purpose. Though we women are natural nurturers, we must submit this gift to God for His guidance on how and when to utilize it. Ask yourself how much of your assistance to a man is fueled by the fear that if you don't make yourself indispensable to him, he'll no longer need you or want you. This is sin. Codependency, enabling—all of these are merely catch phrases to mask what one is really doing, which is stepping over the boundaries of the original assignment and infringing on God's job. God does not need your help. He knows how to handle it.

Think of the women who put their men through college, only to be left behind once that man has gotten on his feet. This is too frequent an occurrence not to render a lesson or two. Sometimes we assist men to our own detriment. One of two things usually happens in these instances. One, the woman who took care of everything in order for him to get his degree is unable to give up the reins now that the man is in the position to take them. So he goes off the moment he finds someone who lets him steer the buggy. Two, the man gets so used to the woman being in charge that he leaves her in charge at home and becomes a workaholic, completely involved in his job where he can run things without contest. The poor woman, who was looking forward to releasing the reins once he was free to take them, plummets to the depths of frustration and disappointment. Feeling doomed to forever watch her husband ignore her needs, the needs of their children, and the needs of their household, she shuts down and switches to automatic pilot, fueled by anger and resentment. As the strain takes its toll on her, he decides that she is no longer attractive and leaves her for a newer, more care-free model. A woman filling a man's shoes is a no-win situation. Why? Because it is out of order—God's order.

"A woman must not wear men's clothing, nor a man wear women's clothing, for the LORD your God detests anyone who does this" (Deuteronomy 22:5 NIV). This Scripture

God wants us to delight in the way in which we were made and not step over the boundaries He so lovingly laid out for our protection and fulfillment. This is the feminine mandate.

should be examined in its context. It is set in the midst of two groups of Scriptures. The preceding verses speak of how to assist in the welfare of others, or take up the slack in the face of another's state of helplessness. The second set of verses, following our dress code verse, distinguishes which opposites did not work well together—such as two different types of seed in the same vineyard, an ox and a donkey plowing together, wool and linen woven together. The point of the whole passage is that each thing has its own unique function. To combine it with something that doesn't match or have the same type of consistency or strength weakens both and disfigures the whole. Though the verse addressing men's and women's attire can be translated literally to address "cross-dressing," we must also look at the larger picture of what God is saying. When women strive to "dress" like men, or men try to "dress" like women, they become at best a caricature of the real thing. God said that we were "good" just the way He made us. He gave men certain strengths that women do not possess. Likewise, women possess certain strengths and gifts that no man will ever be able to effectively imitate.

This was a deliberate move on God's part so that no one would get a big head and make the incorrect conclusion that he or she didn't need the other. The two parts were given different strengths and weaknesses so that when they came together, they would be like a puzzle. The pieces would fit and the picture would be complete. Man and woman equally yoked together, balancing life between the two. Single women, if a man is not present in your life, the Lord Himself will shoulder your load and complete the picture. But married women, He will not assist you in helping a man out of his position or rescue a man who is not fulfilling his duties. He is faithful to fill the gap in your life as you look to Him to be your source while you release your mate into His hands. God wants us to delight in the way in which we were made and not step over the boundaries He so lovingly laid out for our protection and fulfillment. This is the feminine mandate. Let Him go before you, let Him fight your battles. Tone your muscles by loving, not fighting.

So, woman, be free to be a woman, fearfully and wonderfully made, releasing your struggles into the hands of the Lord and the one He has put into your life to shoulder the load. And let that man be a man, even if it kills you to watch. Remember the Scripture where Paul speaks of putting on the armor so that we can withstand trial, "after having done all to stand"? Well, you've done enough, so stand still and let go. Either you trust God to make a man out of your spouse or you don't.

> "You will not have to fight this battle. Take up your positions; stand firm and see the deliverance the LORD will give you, O Judah and Jerusalem. Do not be afraid; do not be discouraged" (2 Chronicles 20:17 NIV).

Dear Heavenly Father, I must admit that I have allowed myself to be swept away by my own expectations. I have invested misguided hope in a man when my hope should have been in You. You alone are my source of peace and joy. You alone can make me fruitful in a way that is pleasing to You and fulfilling to me. As I cast my cares upon You because You care for me, open my eyes to see Your willing participation in my life on a daily basis, even in the little things. I have nowhere else to turn and I am so weary. I admit that I am filled with disappointment, frustration, and resentment. At times I am even angry at You as I begin to buy into the lie that You have failed me. It is really I who have failed myself by demanding more of myself than You do. Help me to relax and let go. Increase my trust in You to take care of the things for

which I feel falsely responsible. Grant me the wisdom to know when I should take hold and when I should let go. Guide me by Your Holy Spirit and do not let me fall prey to my own fearful instincts. As I rest in You, keep that which I have committed into Your hands, now and evermore. In Jesus' name. Amen.

TEN

An Ounce
of Praise

My hero, she breathed
and he slayed yet another dragon
prompted by her praise
he arose to perform exploits
guided by the light of admiration in her eyes
Flexing spiritual muscles
as she waited for him to pray
he climbed
the stairway to heaven
and brought her back a rainbow
for her to wear
and as she told him
that he was her sun
he shone as he had never shone before
and she in turn
opened her spirit
to drink in his rays
and warm her soul
in the fire of his eyes
drinking in his passion for her
she submitted herself to his covering
rejoicing in his love and care
feeling his arms tighten around her
she basked in his embrace
receiving all he chose to bestow
and he
responding to her need of him
dug deeper inside himself
searching for more to give
and as she poured out her adoration of him
he was quick to furnish her

with reasons for more honor
the strength of her love
the softness of her voice
the tenderness of her arms
were trophies
urging him to run with all his might
toward the finish line....
not counting the cost
the pain
the strain
a year seeming as a day
because the reward of her ardor
was so sweet
he would sell all for one whispered confession
of how her heart moved
in his presence
for one glance from her was all it took
to make his world stand still
for her
he lived
for her approval he strove
for her touch he breathed
it was for her
that he had his very being
for the absence of her adulation
was darkness to him
for she
who crowned him king
was his crowning glory...

*M*ichal peered through the window, taking in the procession winding its way into the city of David. It seemed that the farther the crowd advanced, the higher the pitch of their celebration grew. And who should be the biggest culprit of all but her husband, King David? She could not believe his lack of dignity. She could feel the bile rising from her stomach as she watched him leaping and dancing his way right out of his clothing before the Lord. Her mouth tasted as bitter as her heart as she pondered how much she despised him in that moment. She despised him as much as she had once loved him. At this very instant in time, it was hard for Michal to fathom the adoration she had once felt for this man. But perhaps it was because she felt that half of what she'd put out had never been reciprocated.

From the time David had come to work for her father, Michal had loved him. She remembered that when she first saw him, she heard her own sharp intake of breath, for he was altogether lovely in a poetic sort of way. And when he played the harp to soothe her father Saul's senses, she was all the more enthralled. He had this gentle way about him that tugged at her heart, yet he was fierce in war, killing Philistines by the thousands. He was a romantic warrior, the fulfillment of a woman's perfect fantasy. When Saul had offered David her older sister as a bride, her heart sank and then took wing again when he refused. Her feelings for David were all too transparent to anyone in her presence, and soon it was also known to her father how much she loved him. Saul seemed pleased and arrangements were made with the requirement that David slay 100 Philistines and deliver their foreskins for the hand of Michal. David, to prove his desire for Michal's hand, slayed an extra 100 Philistines above the required number, and they were wed.

The honeymoon, however, was short-lived. Saul sought to kill David. Michal, not able to bear the thought of her beloved's death, chose separation instead by helping him to escape. Braving the fury of her father was an easier sentence to endure. However, her last memory of David slipping away into the night was not enough to sustain her in the long years that passed. Her father in his anger had her wed to another man, Paltiel, and there she remained as the years rolled by, with no word from David. He made no attempt to rescue her as he ran for his own life, even after she had ransomed hers in exchange for his.

It was a hard pill for Michal to swallow, but perhaps David had never loved her the way she had loved him. The dawning of this realization birthed a coldness within her. She pulled the shutters of her heart down that day and relegated her affections to safekeeping. Women had no time for these foolish notions. She made the best of her new situation as her life returned to normalcy. Her new husband, though not of her choosing, loved her, and as the years rolled by and thoughts of David grew dimmer, she turned her attentions toward appreciating what was before her.

And then the unthinkable happened. Word came that David had finally triumphed over her father and was headed for the throne. He had ordered for her return. Ordered for her return! For what, she did not know. Another political move? Surely it could not have been out of love. She'd heard that he had acquired other wives. He had even fought for these wives when they were kidnapped. Had he ever fought for her, a woman who had saved his life? No! Instead, he had the nerve to say he had paid for her with 200 Philistine foreskins. Michal wished she had them to throw back at his feet if that was all she meant to him—a mere reminder of a hard-won battle. But at this point nothing could be done; return she must.

Michal couldn't bear to look back as she went. She could hear Paltiel weeping loudly behind her. If she looked back, she knew she would never make it. And so she set her face toward where she was going, clinging to the last shreds of her strength. Struggling to remember her love for David, she shivered from the cold she felt even though it was the hottest of days. She felt like an empty shell the wind could have easily blown through. She was drained; she had nothing left, nothing left to give to one she felt had never given anything to her.

And now, watching him with detached interest as he danced before the Lord in wild abandon, the women singing his praises as he sang praises unto God, it finally hit her. She realized why this scene turned up the heat under the pots of bitterness that simmered in her soul. To David, God had always been more important than her. Israel had always been more important than her. David was a man consumed by his work and his God. She felt separated from him. He always seemed so distracted, lost in thought behind the dark curtains of his heart where only God was allowed to enter in. As a matter of fact, Michal knew that he spent more time worrying over the absence of the ark of God than he had over her. Never had he displayed his love for her in such wild abandon as he did now for the Lord, dancing out of his clothes! And everyone looked on, looked to see what should have been for her eyes alone. Even though David was a splendid specimen of a man, the bitterness in her stomach turned to bile that made her ill, so deep was her distaste for his display. And with that Michal turned from the window; she had seen enough.

Down below, David, none the wiser, danced in elation. The ark of the Lord had come home. This was truly cause for celebration. This was the perfect period to the end of a most tumultuous season in his life. After all his years of running to preserve his life, the struggle was over—he was king, ordained by God. All the pieces had come together, with his family now intact safely within his walls. All was well. Now he could embrace a new beginning for himself and his loved ones. David determined to bless his family and all of his household the moment he stepped across the portal. His cheeks were flushed, his eyes sparkled from the exhilaration he felt. As he stepped into the dimness of his hallway, he was stopped by the energy emanating from one rigid figure coming toward him. His eyes adjusted to view Michal, oblivious to his joy, practically spitting venom through her tight-lipped sneer as she lifted her haughty eyes to him, not even attempting to mask her complete contempt of his behavior. "Well, well, well," she hissed. "A fine sight you are! The king

of Israel—disrobing in the sight of the slave girls of his servants as any vulgar fellow would!"

Michal waited for David to deflate, but he did not. Something, however, did happen. Something indistinguishable
between them changed as he quieted long enough to address
her then, to gently let her know that he had no problem
casting his dignity to the wind in the sight of God. He rejoiced
in his humility before the Lord. But there was one more thing
he knew. If she didn't want to give him honor, he would receive
honor from the very women she scorned. He had no problem
accepting honor elsewhere. None at all. And with that he
walked past her to bless the rest of his house. And that which
Michal thought was dead within her resurrected to die another
death. Something told her she had crossed an invisible line.
Now she had lost him, and she couldn't get him back. She
couldn't get him back because she didn't know which part of
him to grasp in order to even attempt his heart's retrieval. For
she realized too late, as she slipped into the abyss of a loveless
and childless existence for the rest of her days, that though she
had loved him, she had never really known him.

Making the Bitter Sweet

Where do we begin to explain how the communication
breakdown occurs when two people lose their way in a relationship, each accusing the other of being self-absorbed? To
Michal, David only cared about himself. Perhaps David felt
the same was true of her. But the bottom line is that two
wrongs will never make a right. What bridges the gap
between two separated spirits? Understanding. How do we
come to the place of understanding, able to stand under the
protective covering of knowing where the other person is

coming from? To hear Michal's story is to see where her feelings could have been justifiable.

But what of David's side of the story? Perhaps in his mind, he felt it was dangerous to drag Michal into the war between her father and himself. Better to leave her where she was safe until he could get his bearings. He knew what she was used to. He couldn't expect her to be happy about the prospect of being on the run, sleeping in caves and tents for years on end, could he? And now that Saul was dead and things were coming together, there was still the matter of the ark of God being returned to its rightful place. There would be plenty of time to turn his attention toward things on the home front once he took care of first things first. After all, he was responsible for the welfare of a country as well as his own house. The well-being of them all depended on their relationship with God. It was up to him to make certain that everything was done in the right order. These are the things Michal, who was not familiar with the nature of a man, would never have known or understood. She chose to dwell on how her husband's lack of attention was making her feel instead of reaching out to discover what was really going on inside of him. And in the moment that could have changed the tide of their entire relationship, she blew it with words of anger fueled by the pain of her own misunderstanding.

This is the same place where most of us women slip and fall. Instead of realizing that we are internalizing someone else's behavior that usually has nothing to do with us personally, we lash out at the person who we see as the source of our pain. The other person is caught off guard, jolted back to a present of which he was actually oblivious. After all, he was busy slaying his own dragons. As the two stand wondering why they are the recipients of wounds instead of assistance, the chasm between them grows wider. Can you imagine what a different scenario it would have been had Michal, in spite of the way she felt, chosen to keep her com-

---

To be naturally feminine women is to walk in the awareness of our importance. In order to do this, we must have a grasp on the ways of men.

---

plaints to herself until a more appropriate time when she knew David could really hear how she felt?

An ounce of praise would have changed the course of Michal's marriage. If she had greeted David with congratulations for recovering the ark of God, it would have been a different day. He would have included her in his victory. He would have loved her and blessed her. Instead, he moved past her and never looked back. He had others who would give him honor. Remember, ladies, the notion that we can punish a man is laughable. A man will never do without; he will find another source of pleasure. To create a void is to set yourself up to be replaced.

I've mentioned this before, but I would like to take a deeper, more detailed look at this topic because it is crucial to our femininity. To be naturally feminine women is to walk in the awareness of our importance. In order to do this, we must have a grasp on the ways of men.

Here's the biggie. Men need appreciation, honor, respect...worship, in a sense. Awww, I hear you, I hear you! "Well, what about me?" you might say. "When am I gonna get a little respect around here? Why is it always about *their* ego? Men! They just need to grow up!" That may be true, but we've sung that song long enough to know that these comments don't change anything. In other words, you're preaching to the converted. So how do we take this knowledge and put it to use in our lives and in our personal relationships? Let's examine God's heart on this issue. Because we are created in His image, it is natural for all of us to seek praise and adoration. Yes, ladies, we seek it too. We're just a little more subtle with our stuff.

> "Yet a time is coming and has now come when the true worshipers will worship the Father in spirit and truth, for they are the kind of worshipers the Father seeks. God is spirit, and his worshipers must worship in spirit and in truth" (John 4:23 NIV).

> "Ascribe to the LORD glory and strength, ascribe to the LORD the glory due his name. Bring an offering and come before him; worship the LORD in the splendor of his holiness" (1 Chronicles 16:28,29 NIV).

"I will sacrifice a freewill offering to you; I will praise your name, O LORD, for it is good" (Psalm 54:6 NIV).

"Through Jesus, therefore, let us continually offer to God a sacrifice of praise—the fruit of lips that confess his name. And do not forget to do good and to share with others, for with such sacrifices God is pleased" (Hebrews 13:15,16 NIV).

"The king is enthralled by your beauty; honor him, for he is your lord" (Psalm 45:11 NIV).

Now, if we look at this worship thing in the context of women being representative of the church—or the bride of Christ—and husbands or the men in our lives as types of Christ, we can see how the cycle of love and honor goes. God is enthralled by our beauty, and as we worship Him through willing submission and praise, He pours out more and more of His love upon us. He dwells in the midst of our praises. This is understandable. All of us would prefer to be in a place where we were celebrated. Who wants to just be tolerated? Not me! By the same token, God has made us extraordinary creatures, beauteous in every way. Men are enthralled by our beauty until we mar it. But when we shower them with appreciation and words of acknowledgment, submission, and honor, they trip over themselves to pour out even more offerings on our behalf.

Sometimes praise is not an easy thing to offer. That's why God calls us to bring a *sacrifice* of praise of our own free will. Decide to praise even when you don't see a reason to praise. Do it as unto God.

"Let us not become weary in doing good, for at the proper time we will reap a harvest if we do not give up. Therefore, as we have opportunity, let us do good to all people, especially to those who belong to the family of believers" (Galatians 6:9,10 NIV).

Praise, or honor, can be looked at in several different ways, all of them equally important in their context. We are called to worship God in spirit and in truth, meaning that He wants our worship from the inside out. He wants us to say what we mean and do what we say. He doesn't want grudging praise rendered out of obligation; He wants praise that rolls off our lips freely because we really believe that He is worthy to be celebrated. How do we know that He is worthy to be lifted up and honored? Because we know Him. How do we know Him? We know His thoughts because of His Word. His Word reveals who He is and how He feels about us. It tells us of His plans for us. So even if we don't see the manifestation of something we desire in our life right now, one flip through His Word reminds us that it is His intention to bless us with the desire of our hearts. This frees us to praise Him while we wait.

She Who Has an Ear

Broken down into day-to-day relationships, a part of the giving honor to a man is being willing to listen to him, drawing him out and hearing his heart. It's also not criticizing when you don't understand, but simply listening, and praying within that God will give you the right responses if what he shares doesn't quite sit well with you. The man in your life should feel that he can hide his heart and his dreams with you. He should feel that he can tell you anything. Believe me, if he can't tell you, he'll tell the secretary or some other lady friend, and then that woman will have the advantage at winning his heart because she knows him. After the fall, the Bible says that "Adam knew Eve and she conceived." To know someone is to reach the depths of intimacy with him. Something will always be birthed out of intimate sharing. You now carry a piece of that person within you. Some secret, some feeling, some fear—whatever he felt safe enough to deposit into your knowing. He trusted you not to hold his heart for ransom or exploit him by casting his pearls before the eyes of those who wouldn't recognize their value. True intimacy is built when we keep the precious secrets that others have placed in our keeping.

When we understand the heart of God, we can endure even the times of chastening by His hand because we know they are for our own good. When we know the heart of the man in our life, we will be able to stand in the knowledge of his love for us, even if he seems a little preoccupied. Being in tune with his heart and how he thinks and works will give you patience and arrest the temptation to personalize what might be an internal trial he needs to work out on his own.

Listening to and knowing your mate will also help you release him to have his own space with God. It will silence all voices which tell you that you are being squeezed out of the mix, that you are on the outside looking in, that the spot you felt was reserved only for you has been violated by someone with whom you cannot compete. I love the story about Moses going up on the mountain to talk with God and receiving the commandments for the children of Israel. Aaron, his brother, was left down below to watch over the Israelites. As time went on and the natives got restless because Moses wasn't coming back fast enough, Aaron, too, fell prey to being discontent. You can imagine that he felt like a stepchild saddled with all responsibility and no authority. How he must have grumbled in his heart about how Moses got to go up to see God while he was stuck down below with these knuckleheaded people. It just wasn't fair; who died and gave Moses all the clout? Meanwhile, God spent a major part of the forty days that Moses was away giving detailed directions about His plans for Aaron presiding over the priesthood, down to the specific clothes he was supposed to wear! While you're sitting somewhere feeling ignored, God could be talking to that man about you! He might be making plans to bless you big-time. Because of our own insecurities, we sometimes don't get to see the plans that lie in the heart of the man in our lives. We stop them from coming to fruition with our own low expectations, misconceived notions, and the actions that follow.

> "'For I know the plans I have for you,' declares the LORD, 'plans to prosper you and not to harm you, plans to give you hope and a future'" (Jeremiah 29:11 NIV).

> "No eye has seen, no ear has heard, no mind has conceived what God has prepared for those who love him" (1 Corinthians 2:9 NIV).

Know that God is on your side and that He is an advocate you can trust as He deals with the heart of your man. Meanwhile, you can draw closer to God and gather your own information. He will fill in the blanks that your man won't. Sometimes the man in your world just can't express his thoughts and emotions. It is much easier for women to put their finger on exactly what they're feeling and why. We have been gifted with incredible vocal abilities that surpass that of a man's. This is a scientific, physiological fact. Sometimes he won't tell you how he feels, and that's because he can't. The end, by his chromosomes, okay?

Michal didn't know David. Therefore, she did not trust his intentions toward her. And she missed it completely. Here comes her husband, ready to bless her, and she cuts him off at the pass with insults. Men don't usually handle criticism well; they just flee until you get over it. If it occurs too often, they just avoid you altogether and go elsewhere in search of praise. Get the picture? So watch your mouth, my sister. The power of changing how that man relates to you lies in your hands and in your tongue.

The Language of Love

What is it about praise that makes us so reluctant to render it? And this is across the board—woman to woman, woman to man. I came to the conclusion a long time ago that men are kinder to one another than women are. They don't fling a lot of mud. If something is deserving of praise, they just go ahead and punch the other guy in the arm and say, "Hey, great job, buddy!" Actually, I think it's a part of their male ethic, to give honor where it's due. But for women—well! It's a whole different issue. That's because we see praise as a weapon we wield. Praise blesses and liberates people. To withhold praise is to punish. It is to render the other person to the deepest depths of insecurity, misery, and meaninglessness. Withholding praise can be a subtle case of manipulation. To punish is to sin because you have pressed past judging as discernment to judging as rendering a verdict for what you have personally decreed as a sin against you. Only God gets to give that decree and render judgment. To punish as a manipulative device is to sin because you are messing with somebody's will. That also is not your job. When you start stepping on God's toes, you get in trouble.

So the man in your life isn't doing what you think he should be doing? The operative words here are "what you think." You have prayed and prayed, and it seems as if he and

---

Most of the time we as women give when we shouldn't, enabling men to be wimps, or we withhold when we should give, crippling the man from rising up and taking his place.

God have a conspiracy against you because boyfriend is not changing. Perhaps God is waiting for *you* to change. Perhaps He's working on *you* through that knuckleheaded man. Remember, God uses all relationships to shape and mold us, to instill integrity and strength of character within. So expect to be stretched, and check yourself before you start leveling blame. Purpose to praise even when you don't feel like it, because you can't see the whole picture. You don't have the full blueprint for what God is doing *to* you or *through* you.

The pleasure principle in modern society tells us that if it's God, it should be easy and feel good. Well, as Sportin' Life in "Porgy and Bess" said so prolificly, "It ain't necessarily so." There was no pleasure for Jesus in dying on the cross, but He praised anyway, knowing the way He took was necessary to claim the end benefit.

Jesus was willing to praise in every circumstance because He was willing to share the glory with His Father. This is where plenty of us get hung up. We like to feel that we became fantastic all by ourselves. Giving someone else praise means that we have to split a little bit of the glory, kinda like what got Lucifer in trouble in the first place. It means you've got to give that man some credit for you being the woman you've become. And God forbid we do that! He might get a big head. But then again, what's wrong with that? If that's the case, your heads can explode together. Certainly he's become the man he is because of you. And that goes for good or bad. (Uh-oh, I'm in trouble now!) We all want power but we are not willing to take ownership for all that that implies. Most of the time we as women give when we shouldn't, enabling men to be wimps, or we withhold when we should give, crippling the man from rising up and taking his place.

Praise is the language of love. I love the book of Song of Songs in the Bible. Now, here were two people who understood praise! If ever there was a couple in love, they were it. The king and the Shulamite woman were true lovers. They were worshipers. Their sonnets of love were choruses of praise. They took nothing for granted about one another. Oh, your cheeks are like this, and your eyes are like that. Oh, but your neck is so lovely and your teeth are so perfect. Oh, you are so beautiful, my love! Oh, no, it is *you* who is so handsome....My, my, my! It's a wonder they heard what the other was saying, both were so ardent in voicing their affections. Even the women around them wondered what was going on. The king couldn't be all that, could he? And Shulamite declared, oh, yes he was. He was all that—and then some. Shulamite did not have a problem being free with praise for her man whether she was in a crowd or alone. Everybody was going to know that she had a good thing. And in return, he showed up to prove to all who knew her that she hadn't lied.

Some of us are too conscious of all the people who really don't matter in the scenario. Michal was worried about how David looked to the people around him. Those people were not dwelling on David's appearance; they were too busy celebrating themselves to care. When they were finished, they all went back to their own homes to get caught up in their own issues without a backward glance. The same holds true for those in our world today. Most women spend too much time worrying what others around them would think if they were serving or praising their man the way in which they should. They don't want to look like a doormat to their friends. Let me tell you an interesting thing about doormats. Have you ever noticed that a doormat, inside or outside of a house, doesn't usually look dirty even though everybody who enters the house wipes their feet on it? A doormat must be made of some pretty durable stuff, because it takes an extreme amount of wear for a doormat to become worn-out and dirty. But here's the thing about this same doormat. That little square keeps the rest of the house from being sullied. It absorbs everything that could ruin everything inside. I guess that's why the Bible says that the little parts we think are less honorable, we need to treat with special honor (1 Corinthians 12:22,23). The doormat saves the entire house. Think about it. Kind of gives you a new perspective on doormats, doesn't it?

I'll give you a big hint to help you out here and get you unstuck. Stop looking at your mate and seeing him as the husband who doesn't meet your expectations, and instead see him as a man who's doing the best he can. You know what's funny? Most men don't have a bunch of expectations when it comes to women. They just kind of take things as they come. As long as nothing rocks the boat and causes perpetual drama in their kingdoms, they're pretty cool. But women come loaded down with all kinds of qualifiers on how this man should behave. "If he really loves me, then he should prove it." That's what God has been saying to all of us since forever began, but He doesn't beat us up when we fail. He instead invites us to come and reason with Him. The door is always open as far as He is concerned, even if we've let Him down. So who has given us the license to decide when someone is undeserving of praise?

I know what the next big question is: What do *I* get out of this deal? I'll tell you. Praise is as much for you as it is for the other person. Praise is an opportunity to rehearse the good in the other person. It is your way of reminding yourself why you are blessed to have this person in your life. It releases you from harboring past hurts or slipping into bitterness. It releases you to be joyful and releases the one who has been praised to cheerfully give to you. It stirs up the desire within that person to be the best that he can be for you. He longs to rise beyond the heights you've encouraged him to reach because he doesn't want to let you down. That's what you get out of praise.

Now that you've mastered the art of praise, you'll be even more free to revel in worship. As a single woman walking with Christ and being obedient in the area of celibacy, I am always amazed at the number of married women I encounter who struggle with the desire to have sex with their husbands. Now, personally, I have concluded that all of these women never had to endure lack or they would appreciate the gift that is now readily available to them. A preacher once said that married people, who have been given the license to operate their sex drive, don't even know if they want to get in the car, while the single people stand on the sidelines saying, "Well, can we borrow your driver's license?" Some are even willing to settle for a learner's permit at this point. But, seriously, I think that because of Satan's hatred of marriage, this is an area where he wreaks absolute havoc. It is our ignorance of what sex truly is in the eyes of God that causes us to misuse, abuse, and fail to appreciate this gift for what it is.

The Origin of Worship

Sex is a type of worship. Did you know that? Even the heathen know it; that's why orgies were a part of the worship ceremonies for pagan deities. They saw the power associated with rendering all their members as an offering or sacrifice to the one they served, even to the point of death. This was an abomination before God.

On the other hand, Paul encourages us to worship in a way that pleases God, presenting our bodies as living sacrifices, holy and pleasing, unto God—this is our "reasonable service," or "spiritual service of worship," as another translation states (Romans 12:1). In the garden, Adam and Eve were holy and pleasing to God. They were naked and unashamed. They celebrated the glory of God's creation as they beheld one another. Nothing marred the perfection that

God had created within them until they plummeted into the abyss of their own willfulness. Then they ran for cover. The cover conceived separation, separation nurtured secrets, and secrets evolved into mistrust and blame, which gave root to isolation. From there, isolation sprouted territorialism, and territorialism gave birth to war—war between the sexes. Even when men and women married, the war would continue. Though visible weaponry would not be utilized, these invisible weapons of warfare would be more lethal, for they would strike at the inner core of one another's beings. Yes, the celebration was over. Finished. Kaput. What man and woman had shared as the sweet, intimate communion of two spirits became an act of the flesh that lost its original intent.

To understand this, we must first remember once again that many things in the spiritual world are parallel to things in the natural world. Sex is one natural parallel to the spiritual act of worship. The spiritual act of worship began with the atonement process—the purifying of the body, the shedding of blood, the entering into the holy of holies bearing burning coals and incense to present to the Lord. The path of offenses had to be cleared before encountering a Holy God. Not everyone was allowed into the holy of holies, only the priest whom God had chosen. Even for that priest to enter the holy of holies harboring sin was an offense to God that resulted in death. Repentance must be a part of worship. As God responds to our worship, His presence is made real to us. It is before the presence of God that we see ourselves as we truly are. We are then able to confess, voicing our deeds as He sees them. This is true confession. As we see things in the light of God's Word, our minds are changed and the repentance process is complete. We turn away from that sin, never to revisit it again.

As we look at the intimate exchange between a man and a woman, the parallels become clear. When a man knows that he has hurt or offended a woman, his first instinct is to make love because it is difficult for him to vocalize remorse effectively (or so he thinks). It is his way of saying he's sorry. In many ways, a woman's makeup is a reflection of God's heart. Her body and her emotions are a tribute to His heartbeat. Everything about her body is fashioned to nurture life. Her breasts give milk, her arms hold and comfort, and her womb incubates and births living souls into the earth. Her ability to nurture makes her the conduit for the influence that she is. Though everything about her frame is pointed toward giving, God has placed a cavity within her for receiving. But, like God, she finds it hard to receive from man when she is offended. Her body, in a sense, is like the holy of holies. Not everyone can enter into your holy of holies, and unresolved offense can be death to the consummation of the worship or sexual experience.

Even as God gives completely of Himself, He desires to receive our worship. Though He is not incomplete without it, it is His desire. Yet He has requirements for the type of worship He can receive. The offenses that stand between us must be cleared away. Even as He demanded the best of the sacrifice, He demands the best of our praise, holy and unadulterated. We must be cleansed, which we are as we pass through the blood of Jesus Christ. We bring our passion and our praise before Him, and He meets us, engulfing us in His presence.

Purification in the natural begins with bathing, preparing the body to be pleasing to your partner. As men are circumcised and women bleed at the first sexual encounter, this is the passage through the blood in the natural. Virginity is a type of the best sacrifice. Don't fall into condemnation here. Remember, we've already covered God restoring your virginity as you walk before Him in the newness of the life you now possess. I am merely walking you through the blueprint as it relates to the order of worship. The burning coals and incense are now replaced by the passion, appreciation, and praise you shower on one another throughout your intimate encounter. You as a woman feel surrounded by the presence of your mate and vice versa. You are both naked and unashamed, seeing one another as you truly are. You are no longer separated by pretense or offenses. Instead, you are totally yielding, giving everything you have, everything you are, to one another, completely pouring out but being filled at the same time. This is worship in its purest form. Just as we feel spent but satisfied after a worship session with God, this feeling should be mirrored in the natural with your mate.

I must interject here for those single women reading this that it is important to understand how God views sex so that it is not misused. There is right worship and there is wrong worship. Wrong worship brought death to Aaron's sons when they offered the wrong fire and incense before God. To look at this literally, you can say that sex outside of marriage brings about death to our spirits, as well as to our sense of well-being or esteem. In some cases, it brings death to our bodies through sexually transmitted diseases, abortions, and the fatal attractions that are a result of soul ties from the sexual union. Get the picture?

> "The body is not meant for sexual immorality, but for the Lord, and the Lord for the body….Flee from sexual immorality. All other sins a man commits are outside his body, but he who sins sexually sins against

his own body. Do you not know that your body is a temple of the Holy Spirit, who is in you, whom you have received from God? You are not your own, you were bought with a price. Therefore honor God with your body" (1 Corinthians 6:13,18-20 NIV).

"Don't you know that you yourselves are God's temple and that God's Spirit lives in you? If anyone destroys God's temple, God will destroy him; for God's temple is sacred, and you are that temple" (1 Corinthians 3:16,17 NIV).

Wrong worship, like bad perfume, will cling to your clothes and your countenance as you walk under the cloud of condemnation. Long after you've asked God for forgiveness, the sting of sin will remain to trouble you. It is a trick of the enemy to have you fall into fornication, enjoy it for a season, and then revisit you with condemnation long after God has forgotten about it. By the time you meet a godly man, you feel undeserving of his attention because the enemy rises up to accuse you of being a "sinful ole thing." This either makes you freeze up and subconsciously sabotage the relationship, or you end up spilling your guts to the guy (which you shouldn't do; your past belongs to you and God unless it will directly affect his future). This could cause problems because no man wants to know about your previous encounters. He prefers to feel as if he possesses something no one else has had. If he asks you something about your past, you may give him a truthful summation such as, "I was promiscuous before I came to Christ." But spare him the gory details; they are not necessary. Let him see you as God sees you, washed and restored by the blood of Jesus.

In the end, Satan wants to win by suckering you out of something that could have given you joy. He wants to cause problems between you and God, between you and a potential mate. He likes it when your self-esteem is put in the precarious position of dangling between a potential mate's acceptance or rejection of you and your past mistakes. But God doesn't want you going there. He wants to keep you safe

---

From the beginning, Satan's whole M.O. was to steal worship and praise in any form. He comes to steal, kill, and destroy your praise and worship to God, and he comes to steal, kill, and destroy the worship in your bedrooms.

---

from all of that by keeping you surrounded in His will. To indulge in sex before marriage is to be adulterous to the One who is now your husband—God. He is there as a husband to you until His physical arms are manifested in the form of a natural man. He doesn't want you to be robbed of the experience of seeing how He can love you in the meantime.

As you struggle to walk in a life of purity, I encourage you to learn how to worship God. Be creative. Begin by creating an atmosphere for intimacy between you and the Lord. Then turn your attention toward the Lover of your soul. Begin to rehearse and thank Him for His goodness to you. As your praise of Him escalates to the place of adoration, whether in word or song, you will ascend to another place of pouring yourself out before Him. As He meets you in this place, you will experience the deepest kind of satisfaction. You can literally be as spent and refilled from worshiping God as you would be from the natural act of intimacy with a partner. This is God's way of fulfilling your need for becoming one with another as a single person. The more you practice this, the sweeter your times with the Lord will become. This is your special gift to cherish. Worship will also help you get through those difficult times. If you don't direct your worship toward God, you will direct it elsewhere. This is what Satan hopes for. He comes to steal worship from singles by causing them to fall into sin. He comes to steal worship from those who are married by setting up myriad distracting circumstances.

Here is the thing you must know. From the beginning, Satan's whole M.O. was to steal worship and praise in any form. He comes to steal, kill, and destroy your praise and worship to God, and he comes to steal, kill, and destroy the worship in your bedrooms. So he will give you a headache, cause your husband to be insensitive, influence the kids to make you crazy, use the circumstances of the day to wear you down...whatever! He will do whatever he has to do to shut down the ministry of worship in your home. Yes, sex is supposed to be a ministry, partner to partner. It's supposed to be a comfort, an escape from the cares of the day for you both. Small wonder the first thing mentioned after Adam and Eve were put out of the garden was that they made love. Think about it. Sex was not just created for multiplying. It was created to release tension, recenter your soul back to the garden, make the world and all its trouble fade away, and reinvent the oneness between man and woman. It was created to literally tie your souls together. It is communion, the joining of

---

Sex is worship, it is communion, it is ministry, and it is a marital duty ordained by God.

---

your spirits together as you partake of one another even as we are invited to partake of Christ in the symbolic receiving of the bread and the fruit of the vine, absorbing Him fully. In this we are healed, made whole again, and saturated with His life within us. It is a heady experience, but perfectly lawful. God has given us permission to be intoxicated in two ways— to be drunk with the Holy Spirit and to be intoxicated with the love of our mate.

"May your fountain be blessed, and may you rejoice in the wife of your youth. A loving doe, a graceful deer—may her breasts satisfy you always, may you ever be captivated by her love" (Proverbs 5:18,19 NIV).

"How delightful is your love, my sister, my bride! How much more pleasing is your love than wine" (Song of Songs 4:10 NIV).

"May your breasts be like the clusters of the vine, the fragrance of your breath like apples, and your mouth like the best wine. May the wine go straight to my lover, flowing gently over lips and teeth. I belong to my lover, and his desire is for me" (Song of Songs 7:8-10 NIV).

We belong to the Lord, and His desire is for us. Likewise, wives belong to their husbands. A man's desire is for his wife, and vice versa. Understanding that your body no longer belongs to you is important. Don't get all excited—his body doesn't belong to him anymore, either.

"The husband should fulfill his marital duty to his wife, and likewise the wife to her husband. The wife's body does not belong to her alone but also to her husband. In the same way, the husband's body does not belong to him alone but also to his wife. Do not deprive each other except by mutual consent and for a time, so that you may devote yourselves to prayer. Then come together again so that Satan will not tempt you because of your lack of self-control" (1 Corinthians 7:3-5 NIV).

Sex is worship, it is communion, it is ministry, and it is a marital duty ordained by God. To withhold it in order to punish your mate is sin. Get rid of the offense. "'In your anger do not sin': Do not let the sun go down while you are still angry, and do not give the devil a foothold" (Ephesians 4:26,27 NIV).

Talk. Communicate. Let your husband know your needs. Influence him to become a better lover. Let him know that making love begins at the beginning of the day, not one moment after the lights go out. Here's a fact: The average man is like a microwave oven, heating up fast. Women, however, are like Crockpots, coming slowly to a boil. Understanding these differences goes a long way in the bedroom. With understanding, adjustments can be made to accommodate both of your needs. Share with him your emotional and physical needs along with what it takes to please you. He is interested, believe me, but it's more than likely he will never ask. Or he'll assume, based on previous experience, that every woman's body works the same way. But you have been created to be uniquely you. You have your own personal body combination, as my friend P. B. Wilson calls it. Teach him your combination. Now, don't lecture the man; let the learning session be fun. Ask God to give you an inventive way to do it. Because God blesses the marriage bed, it's a good idea to invite Him into it. After all, He knows both of your personal body combinations. Let God instruct you on how to please one another.

As the two of you come together in unity of spirit, soul, and body, God is well-pleased and glorified. As He is glorified, you are blessed to receive an extraordinary gift—a glimpse of what your union with the ultimate Bridegroom, Jesus Christ, will be like when you are joined to Him in the heavenlies. As your pleasure is heightened to a crescendo in the marriage bed, you are afforded for a moment a foretaste of the ecstasy you will feel throughout eternity. That's why we'll need glorified bodies. These little mortal bodies wouldn't be able to stand it!

Now, for those of you who have had problems since I started talking about this because you don't find sex an enjoyable experience at all, or even at times a painful experience, let's talk about this. Several things could be the cause. One is mental conditioning. Perhaps when you were a little girl, sex was spoken of as a "dirty thing" at your house, and you were never taught to see it as a celebration according to God's design. It was perhaps even taboo to speak of it. You learned that sex was a deep, dark secret, something that you *had* to do in marriage, so you would just grit your teeth and bear it when the time came. Or perhaps you are still tormented by memories of sexual abuse. But God *can* heal your heart and your mind and make the beauty of His design for sex a reality to you. And keep in mind that you might actually be experiencing a sexual dysfunction due to hormones or a physical problem. Do not hesitate to seek medical help. There are doctors who specialize in this area, and you should consult with your regular physician or gynecologist if you suspect such a problem. Do not allow Satan to steal the worship at your house! It should be an enjoyable experience for both of you.

As the saying goes, "When the praises go up, the blessings come down." Why do so many men want sex all of the time? Perhaps because of the increase of outward stimuli via the visual and audio media there is an added dimension of pressure to men that accelerates their hormonal makeup and stimulates their need for physical satisfaction. Whatever the case, it is safe to say their need comes from a place of desiring self-fulfillment—versus God, who craves our worship because He deserves it. He is pouring out blessings to us constantly, therefore He *should* receive worship ad infinitum. In tying this together, men are made in the image of God, therefore they want what God wants, though from different motivations. God wants our worship all the time. Our worship is the pronouncement and affirmation of His power. Men also continually look for affirmations of their power. Some are even willing to cheat for it or pay for it, if you get my drift. But God patiently awaits our turning toward Him; He will not be distracted from us. As our worship goes up to Him, He opens the windows of heaven and pours out blessings we won't have enough room to receive. Too tired to worship? Have you ever noticed that when you just press your way and begin to worship, once you get going you get a burst of energy and you feel revitalized? That's because energy releases energy. The same principle applies to exercise. Medical doctors even agree that an active sex life takes years off of people and keeps them youthful. True worshipers should expect God's promise that their strength will be renewed. They will mount up with wings like eagles, run and not be weary, walk and not faint (Isaiah 40:31). So determine to worship, for God's sake, for your husband's sake, and for your own sake.

Remember that an ounce of praise can turn the tide of a marriage and give it a refreshing. So press past feelings. Press past anger. Forgive and forgive again as you would have God forgive you. Press past the weariness. Press past the veil of your own previous perceptions and enter into the place of blessing. Become enfolded in the arms of God, caught up in the rapture of His love for you now being poured out through the body of the one He has chosen to be the natural mani-festation of Himself in your life—your husband. Respond to your husband as unto God, and God will meet you there and bless you both. Remember the incense that was carried into the holy of holies? As you know, incense is quite pungent. Its smell lingers in the air long after it's finished burning. Well, good worship is like that. It lingers like costly incense, per-meating the way you respond to one another long after the worship is over. For this reason, worship will resonate beyond your bedroom walls and affect the lives of your children as they bask in the security of the love that is made apparent between you and your mate. Truly, this is a house where the virtue that emanates from worship will be made evident as husband and child arise to call you "Blessed." This is reason enough to give worship in all things.

> "Each [woman] should give what [she] has decided in [her] heart to give, not reluctantly or under compul-sion, for God loves a cheerful giver. And God is able to make all grace abound to you, so that in all things at all times, having all that you need, you will abound in every good work" (2 Corinthians 9:7,8 NIV).

Dear Heavenly Father, as I bow before Your throne, teach me to worship. In thought, in word, in deed, teach me to worship. In every way, teach me to worship. Release my tongue to render praise, to give honor where honor is due. Fill me with

delight every time I bless someone with praise. Help me to help others celebrate the gifts and the blessings You grant to all of Your children. Forgive me for using praise and worship as a tool of punishment by withholding them. Cleanse me from anger and the pain of offenses. Help me not to hold grudges and seek to strike back at the hearts of those who wound me, whether knowingly or unknowingly. Help me to cleanse myself and pass through the blood once again, as many times as it takes to release me from everything that binds me from being free to worship. Guide me to the holy of holies. Surround me with Yourself as I lift up praise and honor to You. And as You engulf me with Your Spirit, help me to share that which You release over me with others I encounter when I leave Your intimate presence. Let me take You with me throughout every room of my home, my workplace, and anywhere my feet touch. Give me the unction to render praise. In Jesus' name. Amen.

The Reward of Virtue

He watched her from afar off
savoring her special brand of poetry
etched in every step she took
full of grace
vibrating with strength
a reed in the wind
bowing down
but always rising again
there was something about her...
he took her in as she extended her arms
willowy and gentle
possessing secret power
not obvious to the undiscerning eye
her hands wiped
brows fevered with fear and trepidation
and healed them
her touch as cool as her comforting words
soothed those uncertain
and gave sight to the blind
she moved soundlessly through confusion
leaving peace in her wake
while those before her were warmed by her eyes
and the tenderness of her smile
yet strangely moved
even changed
by her appearing
unexplainable as it were
she left no one the same
so profound
was her influence
and though many could not put their finger

on the exact word
       that rearranged their hearts
              they were sure of the source
it was her
       something about her
for long before she was announced
       her presence was known
              it was felt
the air changed
       her virtue saturated
              the atmosphere
       and brought rest
              to tongues too busy
                     hands too weary
       minds too troubled
it was her
       something about her
not heralded but recognized
              drawing like a magnet
              all those thirsty
                     for refreshing
       her spirit gave them drink
and far more times than she knew her closeness was enough
              to set the captive free
       to release those with severed wings
              to take flight
       and as she laughed in delight
              they soared upon the music
                     of her exultation
       until they reached their destination
returning to roost

in the cool of her shadow
until she urged them on again
and as they rose
they carried her with them
tucking her in a safe place inside themselves
that they could revisit
time and time again
for in the end the power they found to fly
was wrapped inside her prayers
coaxed forth by her faith
birthed by
her...
there was something about her...

$\mathscr{A}$s she kissed the last sweet cheek and turned out the light, her thoughts were already on tomorrow. She would rise early to prepare the day to meet her family, but for now she would sleep. The next day, rising with the dawn, she drank in stolen moments with her Maker, refreshing herself in His presence, drawing strength from His hands to give to those who awaited her. And give she did—encouragement to her spouse and wisdom to her children, readying them for the encounters of the day as it unfolded. At the last farewell she turned to the task at hand, creating an oasis for their return at the day's end. And as the world outside her door greeted her, she chose her words and steps well, leaving admiration and encouraged spirits along her path.

As the children grew and her breasts grew vacant from babies, her arms changed direction and embraced the needy. She taught her daughters the ways of a woman by example as she set her hands to spin and weave their provisions and regulate the affairs of her house. By her side, her sons learned the value of hard work as she planted vineyards and they rejoiced as a family in the time of reaping. And as they grew into men and women, leaving her to cleave to their spouses, her arms were filled with the praises of her husband and all they had sown that was now bearing fruit. He, reflecting on the life they had made together, saw her in every step he took, silently urging him on with a touch, a look, a tender caress that said all it needed to say—and more. Together they had built a safe place for their love and a sound harbor for those who needed to visit. Both could testify that neither was the source of all they possessed, for they were empowered by One much greater than themselves. And as they drank from Him, they refilled each other daily, drawing strength to live and love again.

Seize the Day

Ah, the Proverbs 31 woman. Ain't she somethin' else? Makes you tired just thinking about her, doesn't she? For many who read Proverbs 31, a feeling of awe settles over them. Or perhaps consternation is a better word as one scratches her head and wonders how she could ever hope to live up to such a lofty example of womanhood. I mean, how many things can a woman possibly do in the course of one day? It seems the more time I have, the less I achieve. For me personally, I have no husband, no children, no strict nine-to-five job, and yet my day is always crammed to the limit. I fall into bed exhausted at the end of the day, rehearsing a list of all the things still unfinished. Even as we speak, I am up writing this at three in the morning because somehow the day got away from me. I can't imagine adding a husband and children to the mix. I tip my hat to those who juggle all of these different facets of life. I look at my sister who has opted to remain home with her newborn child and maintain a home for her husband, and truly, her plate is full and over-flowing. I wonder how single mothers do it. And yet at the end of the day, we all have a testimony to the faithfulness of God meeting us in the midst of our own unique situation.

So how did the Proverbs 31 woman do it? According to Scripture, she propped up her husband, she sewed, she wove fabrics, she cooked, she got up at the crack of dawn, she bought fields, and she planted a vineyard! Check that out—not some little herbal garden outside the kitchen window, a vineyard! She traded with the merchants, did charity work, decorated her house, and made sure that her family had winter provisions ahead of time. She still had time to set a romantic atmosphere in her bedroom and look gorgeous for her husband, who, by the way, she made look good to all his peers in the gates on top of all this. You kind of get a picture of her not having a strand of hair out of place in the midst of it all, too. Kind of like a "Leave It to Beaver" mother, but on a higher level. I mean, June Cleaver always looked flawless, didn't she? Dinner was always ready, the house was always clean....We watched those shows and grew up with the best of intentions, only to find out that life was not a television show in any sense of the word. Somehow houses got dirty, dinners got burned, children got out of control, and men weren't so helpful, after all. That's when we threw up our hands, feeling powerless and hoping that when the chips "fell where they may," that they would, by some divine interven-tion, fall in the right place. Enter the serpent, stage left, to hiss in our ear, "Where is the reward for being a woman?" and you've got a great case for deep disgruntlement.

Let me comfort you. The Proverbs 31 woman did not achieve all of this in a day. The achievements listed were all the things that she accomplished throughout the span of her years, in the different seasons of her life. She was not Super-woman. She was a real woman just like all of us, living, learning, and unfolding along the way. Plus, she did have servants, and believe me, I can tell you from experience what a difference an extra pair of hands makes. Whenever I go to Africa to visit my dad, I wonder why I live in America. My father has servants—a house steward, a cook, a driver, a laundry person, and others who come and go to perform various functions. My sisters who live there have nannies who assist them with their children. Believe me, this is the only way that any woman I know can keep a spotless house, have delicious meals ready on time, and still look like a breath of fresh air, smiling when her husband arrives home. So give yourself a pat on the back. You're managing just fine!

The Proverbs 31 woman was called a virtuous woman. In the Hebrew, the word "virtuous" literally means "excellence," while the word "virtue" means "force." You, as a woman, never have to demand respect—just be excellent. No one can argue with excellence. Excellence is a force because excellence demands respect. A woman of excellence is a force to be reckoned with. This was the Proverbs 31 woman. She planned her work according to her understanding of her purpose. She recognized the seasons in her life, and she embraced them. Here's the secret—she understood that you can have it all, you just can't have it all at the same time. This releases you to live in the moment and to enjoy it fully.

So right now, perhaps, you're in the trenches, trying to carve out a career. The rest of your life is…well, you don't have a life, or so you think. So realize that maybe right now it's the season for career planting. God is able to keep what is committed to Him (2 Timothy 1:12). Give Him the rest of your life. It will still be there when you get back. Or perhaps you're up to your eyebrows in diapers and baby formula, and you feel that you have no identity other than Mommy. Trust me, children grow up and get on with their lives sooner than any mother cares for them to. Or maybe you're enduring making uncomfortable adjustments in your life in order to accommodate your husband's aspirations. This, too, shall pass, and there will be rewards if you stick with it. Be excellent in all these things.

> "There is an appointed time for everything. And there is a time for every event under heaven" (Ecclesiastes 3:1 NASB).

> "He has made everything appropriate in its time" (Ecclesiastes 3:11 NASB).

Think about how quickly a year passes. No matter how long we think it is taking for our change to come, it always seems to arrive sooner than we are ready for it. I believe it is the trick of the enemy to rob us of peace and joy in our lives during these moments. One who has a sense of destiny and purpose stays centered, awaiting the cues that lead her to the next season. Jesus said He had to do the work of the One who sent Him while it was day, for the night would come when no man could work (John 9:4). Therein lies the next clue. He was centered on the instruction He received from above. This is where the subtle difference lies that gets us off-track and leads us down the garden path, conversatin' with the serpent, nibblin' on all his tasty little fabrications.

To live your life according to what you, or those around you, think you should be doing is to live a life of frustration. You will always set the bar for yourself at some lofty level too high for you to reach. But as you seek God to find out His expectations of you from day to day, you will find yourself released to rejoice in exactly where you are. That is when you begin to sense the power of your position. God plants us where we are needed. As we respond to His call and apply ourselves to what He has placed before us, we become a "force" to be reckoned with.

For Everything There Is a Season

So for a season, He has dubbed you with the title of "mother." For that season, motherhood is a powerful thing. How you wield your power during that time will have major consequences or incredible rewards. Or maybe you've been called to be a single woman, for more seasons than you care to count. I beg to correct you—it's one season. A season is not predicated on time by days. It is determined by the course of nature completing its cycle or by what needs to be accomplished coming to a conclusion. And then we move on. Allow Him to finish what He has begun in you. As you yield to His hand molding and making you into an incredible woman, you will be a "force" to be reckoned with. But it will be according to His design, for a use yet to be disclosed to you if you're not already beginning to walk in it. Enjoy your life now, for there will be days when you will look back and long for just one day to yourself again.

Perhaps you are in a season of adjustment in a marriage, clinging to pieces of yourself and fighting for your own space within the confines of the oneness to which you've been called to aspire. He's so different. What once was fun is now hard work. When will it end? And where is the reward for losing yourself? Yet what if Jesus had asked that? Where would we all be now? But this season, too, will blossom into spring as you learn how to blend and harmonize, balancing your strengths and weaknesses between each other, learning one another's rhythm, filling in each other's spaces. It will become a concert you both can enjoy, but for now it is a season of growth. Growth is a stretching, painful thing. Breaking through the soil of our own hang-ups, baggage, and predeterminations into the light of God's will costs us some things we'd rather cling to along the way. But growth will bear fruit at the end of the day.

We live in such an instant gratification, quick-fix society. It is easy to be convinced that you gotta have it all...right now! But if we had it all right now, where would we go from here? Someone asked me the other day what the average life span was of a person. So I did some calculations based on an average of the world's mortality rate and came up with the age of fifty-five years. Then I was asked, "What happens next?" "You die," I replied. "And then what happens?" I responded, "You go to be with the Lord." "And how long do you live there?" came the next question. "Forever!" I said. "What about everybody else?" "Well," I said, "everybody lives forever somewhere, in heaven or in hell." "So," my friend said, "the average life span is forever, but we are stuck in the now." Wow! I had to sit and chew on that for awhile. It is so true. We have got forever to evolve from being single women to wives to mothers to businesswomen to someone who makes her mark on society. Forever! To be stuck in the now of your existence is to be rendered powerless. "Where there is no vision the people perish: but he that keepeth the law, happy is he" (Proverbs 29:18 KJV).

What law does that verse speak of? The law of your personal, God-ordained purpose. Do you recall the story of Jesus walking down a street one day when a woman who had been plagued by an issue of blood pressed her way through the crowd to see Him? Only able to touch the hem of His garment, she went for it and was healed. But He stopped. He sensed that virtue had left His body. The "force," or power, left His body and healed this woman. We are called to walk in virtue like that. Jesus was smack-dab in the center of His purpose. He knew what His mission statement was. He didn't spend time moaning about how long He was going to have to spend hanging out with a bunch of people who didn't get it or having to deal with this unappreciative group over here. He didn't whine about how long He was going to have to live hand-to-mouth. He didn't count the days until He could leave all this drama behind and get back to His throne in heaven. It had been so nice up there—if only these people knew who He really was. And He didn't stress about how long He was going to have to remain single, battling the flesh, when He had fine women hanging all over Him, washing His feet with their hair and carrying on like they did. Now, don't get crazy—Hebrews 4:15 tells us that Jesus can relate to everything we go through because He was tempted in all areas, yet He did not sin. The bottom line is that He could have had a million complaints, but He had none. He understood the value of what He was doing in His season. Because of this, He was a "force" for healing, deliverance, and salvation. The virtue flowed out of Him and touched even those He wasn't focused on because He was consumed with His call. It even emanated from His clothing, so saturated was He with divine purpose.

We, too, must be saturated with our purpose as women. Only then will the serpent be rendered silent when we understand the value of our call. Young's Literal Translation of the Bible says that when God confronted Eve about eating the fruit, she said that the serpent caused her to forget. She forgot who she was! She forgot what she was created for and went in search of prizes she could have received freely from God, if only she had done her job. Instead, she forfeited all that she had because she forgot her worth. When you rejoice in who you are, it heals those around you. I noticed that when I decided to get happy as a single woman, everyone

A woman who knows who she is is a powerful tribute to femininity.

around me stopped questioning me about when I was going to get married. Though it is a desire of their heart to see me married, it is now their desire for different reasons. Whereas before it was based on a happiness issue, now they feel that I would make some man a great wife because I am a blessing who should not be missed. While the questions pertaining to my marital status used to be a thorn in my flesh, they have been replaced by admiration for how I have embraced my life as a single woman. Others are blessed to learn from my example that the words "single" and "happy" can have a peaceful coexistence. A woman who knows who she is is a powerful tribute to femininity.

Have you ever met a woman and just knew that she was a mother? She just had this *mother* thing about her—a soft glow, a satisfied expression, a gentle and giving heart, and...well, she was a *mother* to everyone around her. A mother's heart is a beautiful thing. People are drawn to it. It is needed and desired in every area of life. Deborah, judge over Israel, was called the mother of Israel. I'm sure it was her nurturing way which won her that title, and in it there was honor. The people willingly followed her.

Ruth was a single woman, freshly widowed, who entered into a season of caring for her mother-in-law in a foreign land. She was honored richly for performing this seemingly inconspicuous task. People in the community spoke of her virtue. She was a "force" in her community because she answered God's call to follow Naomi to Israel and forsake her own identity, family, and familiar surroundings to do what? Glean wheat in a field? Now, we would see that as downright menial. But God saw it as a season of placement. Every day with God is not guaranteed to be a tiptoe-through-the-tulips kind of day. In some cases He allows hardships to compel our purpose into fruition. It was in that same field that Ruth was spotted by a wealthy man, Boaz, who later became her husband and gifted her with a child who would be the grandfather of David, king of Israel. So remember, everything that has happened in your life has contributed to making you the person you are today.

The Waiting Game

As Mary waited for the time when she would be married to Joseph, she rejoiced in being a handmaiden of the Lord.

She was rewarded with a visitation from God Himself, overshadowed by the Holy Spirit, and became the mother of Jesus Christ, Savior of the world. Talk about being a "force"! We as women are all called to birth something that will affect change for the better in the lives of those around us. Mary was a single woman, yet not one who bemoaned her fate. She was available to God and, because of this, He gave her a special honor. He longs to give us all that honor, to fill each one of us with Jesus Christ to overflowing, so that His virtue may flow out of us to touch, to heal, and to deliver. But as with any pregnancy, the birthing of unadulterated virtue takes time.

Abigail had to spend many years married to a fool. Yet she accepted the character of her husband for what it was and learned to live accordingly as unto God. She did not allow it to rob her of her virtue. Because she embraced her season, it liberated her to release what God had placed within her—outstanding character and wisdom. This paved the way for the moment that would steer her around the corner of her destiny. As she walked in her calling as the wife of a fool, acting to preserve his best interest, she walked into her new future as the wife of David, king of Israel. God was her source of deliverance. He honored her obedience to be the best wife she could be in spite of what she suffered. I've shared her story with you in an earlier chapter, but I'm repeating it here to make a different point. Abigail dealt with her unpleasant circumstances with grace, and in the end she received honor. I hope you're beginning to see a pattern here.

I've shared with you the story of the prominent woman of Shunem in the book of 2 Kings, chapter four. She took it upon herself to feed the prophet Elisha every time he passed by. Finally, perceiving Elisha to be a man of God, she decided to prepare a guest room for him so that he would have a place to make himself comfortable whenever he passed by. Grateful for her generosity, Elisha asked what he could do for her in return. No request came to mind, so she said nothing. After she went away, Elisha questioned his servant as to what would be a suitable gift for this woman. The servant mentioned that she had no children. So Elisha had the woman come back and told her that she would have a child at that same time next year. The King James Version says, "At this season...according to the time of life" she would have a son (verse 17). The woman asked him not to lie to her. But true to Elisha's word, it happened just as he had said.

This story is interesting because motherhood was a big thing in Israel. It was a reproach *not* to bear children. Yet when this woman was asked what Elisha could do for her, she said nothing. She had graciously accepted her life as it was, giving where she had opportunity to give and finding her blessing in blessing others. This is powerful because obviously she had learned to be content in spite of her longing. In fact, she was so content that it wasn't even evident to the prophet what was lacking in her life! Her life was full, vibrating with purpose as she anticipated the needs of others. And here came Elisha, telling her that according to the time of life, she would have a son. God moves in our lives according to the time of life, according to the completed cycles of our days, as we master joy and contentment where we are, walking in the understanding of who we are right here, right now. Seeing the incredible value in our position no matter what it is at this moment in time, it completes the full picture of God's perfect design and opens the door for us to enter into new and exciting experiences.

Though we may be blessed, none are exempt from trouble. Several years later, this same woman held this same child in her arms and watched him die. However, she didn't freak out. She didn't rail at the heavens and at God, asking Him why He would play such a cruel trick on her, making her wait forever for a child only to snatch him away from her. No, she did what she had to do. Placing the child on his bed, she shut the door behind her. She didn't even tell her husband what had happened; she just asked him for a donkey to go visit the man of God. When he asked her why she needed to go now, she answered, "It *will* be well," and then went on her way. She didn't stop to say, "Our son is dead in there on the bed." She said nothing more! Can you stand it? How many of us would have been able to say, "It will be well," at a time like that? When she approached Elisha, she bent down and took hold of his feet, and he could see that she was deeply troubled. This is when we find out how much having a child had meant to her all along. She said to Elisha, "Did I ask you for a son? Didn't I tell you not to deceive me?" In other words, "Don't set me up for heartbreak! I had sorted out my life and was doing fine before this. This is a tragedy I cannot accept because I didn't invite it. Now you must fix it, and I'm not leaving here without you."

While this woman was able to release the desire for a child before she had one, things were different for her after her child arrived in the world. The heart of a mother rose up to fill its purpose—preserving the life of her child. Though fiercely determined, she handled the situation in the same gentle way she handled everything else. Elisha responded by following her home to heal her child. As her son was returned to her, she fell at his feet, bowed before the man of God, took her son in her arms, and went out, ready to pick up where she had left off. She remained submitted to her husband and the man of God in her attitude as well as her posture throughout the whole ordeal. She did what only a mother can do.

A friend of mine shared with me the story of her son falling off a cliff while he was camping with friends from college. After a perilous rescue ordeal, he was transported to the hospital in a comatose state. Meanwhile, she flew from Chicago to Washington state, marched into his room as only a mother could, and yelled at the top of her lungs, "Mark, get up!" And guess what? He snapped right out of that coma! Yes, a mother is a force to be reckoned with, and that's why Satan tries so hard to devalue motherhood.

A Woman of Excellence

Ladies, there are no small parts to play when it comes to the career of being a woman. Each one of us has been carefully crafted, intricately designed by God, to fulfill what He views a crucial call in the big picture of this thing we call life. There's a popular saying, "Everybody has their own movie, and everybody gets to write their own script." But in actuality, that is not true. That is what the serpent wanted Eve to do, and it got her and Adam in trouble. What started off as a classic love story, prime for Masterpiece Theater, turned into a real-life drama with terrible consequences. Whenever we seek power without yielding to authority, we will reach the end of the story. The real allegory is that life is one big movie, God wrote the script, He is the director, and we all have our part to play. If we follow His direction, the story is beautiful. But if everybody starts to do their own thing, the result is chaos, a confused audience, and ultimately a bad review.

You were created on purpose to be what you are as a woman. You are the period at the end of your loved one's sentence. Without you, life would be a question. A man spends his entire life looking for his missing rib. There is something missing within him, and you are it—the missing piece that completes the circle of love and well-being in his world. Children are comforted by the ability to return to the first security they once knew, to be fed and nurtured by your warmth and softness. This is all part of God's incredibly thoughtful design when He fashioned you to be uniquely you.

> "For Thou didst form my inward parts; thou didst weave me in my mother's womb. I will give thanks to thee, for I am fearfully and wonderfully made; wonderful are thy works, and my soul knows it very well. My frame was not hidden from Thee, when I was made in secret, and skillfully wrought in the depths of the earth. Thine eyes have seen my unformed substance; and in thy book they were all written, the days that were ordained for me, when as yet there was not one of them. How precious also are Thy thoughts to me, O God! How vast is the sum of them! If I should count them, they would outnumber the sand..." (Psalm 139:13-18 NASB).

Well, if you ever feel like no one is thinking of you, know that you are on the mind of God, 24/7, all day, all night, and any other eternal time that we don't know about. He ordained the seasons of your life as a single, as a wife, as a mother, or as a business mogul, plotting them out very carefully according to what He knew you could handle. Can you imagine if all four seasons were mixed together? We would never know how to dress! We've experienced a little of this lately with all the strange weather we've been having in the world. People have been getting ill as their bodies find it difficult to adjust to the escalating and plummeting temperatures. God knows that in order to operate at peak performance, we need smooth transitions and balance. Think of how a plane lands. God forbid if we just dropped from the sky! Well, you know the end result of that—death.

That is what made the virtuous woman in Proverbs 31 a force, or "a woman of excellence," as another translation calls her. She planned according to her purpose. I'm sure there was a season when she nurtured her babies at her breast and she didn't run all over the place trading with the merchants. It was her season for being a mother. As her children grew older, she added tasks in which they could be included. This served a twofold purpose—she was training them to embrace responsibility and learn the ways of a responsible mate while at the same time adding income to their home. She took the time to plan her household duties to accommodate the needs of her husband, equipping him to be the best he could be. When a man's house isn't together, his head is not together, either. She made certain that his house was in order, and this was apparent in his character. He was able to maintain his status as a man of integrity outside of the home.

As the children grew older and more self-sufficient, she found other interests to fill her time in a worthwhile manner. She invested in the lives of those who were poor or needy. In the end, everything she did was done in excellence because she responded to each season of her life with the appropriate action. General Motors has a slogan: "Do one thing, do it well." I cannot say it any better. A woman of virtue is excellent because she does one thing at a time, according to the season and her purpose, and she does it well. She plans her work and works her plan. She disciplines herself to remain focused on the task at hand until it is completed. She divides the necessary from the extraneous and does not bow to false obligations. She knows when to stop and allow herself to heal for the sake of herself and those around her. Take the time to be a whole woman, and do it well. "Therefore do not be anxious for tomorrow; for tomorrow will take care for itself. Each day has enough trouble of its own" (Matthew 6:34 NASB).

Yes, Satan would love to see us running around looking like chickens with our heads cut off, jacks of all trades and masters of none, making ten promises and keeping not one of them. He wants us to have an active record of being a disappointment on all fronts, to our mates, to our friends, to our children, and to ourselves. Then at the end of it all, after he spurs us on to peak hysteria, and as we fall down in an exhausted heap, he looks at us in disgust and sneers, "Fine example of womanhood you are! No wonder no one can take you seriously." So take a deep breath and say to yourself, "I promise to take one day at a time, and do one thing at a time." What is the reward of virtue? Being able to view your handiwork at the end of the day and to receive praise from God as He says to you, "Well done, good and faithful [servant]; you were faithful with a few things, I will put you in charge of many things, enter into the joy of your master" (Matthew 25:21 NASB).

You see, ultimately, it is not about the praises of man, though those are nice to have. It is really about the approval and blessing of our Master, our Heavenly Father. When we please Him in all that we do, even if it is just in a few things, joy and blessing are the end benefits. "It is the blessing of the

Lord that makes rich, and He adds no sorrow to it" (Proverbs 10:22 NASB).

It is His blessing that truly affirms us. It comes with no added demands or fine print, just floods of well-being. That is true wealth.

Do we as women need men? Of course we do. To say we don't would be unscriptural, but let us put the word "need" into perspective. We need men because God said so, not because we would die without them. No, they are not the air that we breathe. You can exhale now—inhale...in, out, in, out...doesn't that feel good? And not a man was in sight! "The LORD God said, 'It is not good for the man to be alone. I will make a helper suitable for him'" (Genesis 2:18 NIV).

Now, because woman was taken out of man and is a derivative of man, it stands to reason that God meant that it was not good for *either* to be alone. The Hebrew word for woman is *ishshah*; the word *ish* means "man." Some translators feel that *ishshah* may come from a root word meaning "soft." So we are soft, deriving from man, with a womb. I like what one minister said—that women are not the opposite sex of a man, they are the corresponding sex. To say that we are opposite is to suggest that we are adversaries when God designed us to be complements. Correspondents in the news media fill in the gaps for one another. They are usually in two different locations reporting what is happening so that the viewer gets the whole picture. God created us different by design for the sake of the whole picture. If both of us were alike, one of us—man or woman—would not be necessary. Therefore, it is safe to conclude that men and women need one another— as friends, as siblings, as mates, and as lovers. We balance out and complete one another.

This is why I encourage single women to have a healthy network of platonic male friends. You need to learn a lot about men in order to have an enduring relationship with that one special person. True friendship, minus the pressure associated with a committed, romantic relationship, is the best way to learn how men think, feel, and behave in various situations. There are rich friendships to be had with men. They are loyal, honest, and refreshing. They share another view of life and offer interesting alternatives to problems. I have had the blessing of having a solid network of male friends over the years. Though I have not dated anyone for several years, I feel no male void in my life. I have watched my own brothers Ian, Okuru, and Edward go through the ups and downs of their own relationships and know that men also have their struggles, often on a much deeper level than women. For instance, we seem to bounce back faster from disappointment.

Though they are all in their own relationships, Daryll, Jeff, and David have listened to me cry, coaxed me out of bad relationships, and hovered over me protectively for years. They deserve a special blessing for all I've dragged them through, yet they always hung in there, never afraid to tell me when I was being absolutely ridiculous. Joel keeps me honest, Tony makes me think, Jerry makes me laugh, and there are others, but these are my core. They've been my big brothers and supportive friends. The women in their lives have been gracious sisters to allow us to share time and confidences, and I am the richer for it.

So many women have never taken the time to just be friends with a man, and this is a foundational necessity for having a successful marriage. Your husband should be your best friend. You've got to like that man when you don't feel in love with him. You must have things in common that you enjoy mutually outside of the bedroom, or you will struggle all of your days. So learn to enjoy men just because. When men sense that you like them, they will bend over backward for you. Otherwise it is war. They stiffen, dig in their heels,

The bottom line on this femininity thing? Women need men, women need one another, but most of all women need God. After all, we were really created for Him.

and become difficult to deal with in every area of life—whether it be work or buying something at the cash register—when they sense you have a negative attitude toward the male gender. So learn to embrace men for who they are. Don't take everything so personally. Know that their idiosyncrasies were placed there on purpose to make all women collectively better.

Recently, I was in a truck working on the filming of a television commercial with a bunch of men from the production company. I was telling them about this book, and all of the men were keenly interested in the topic. Their eyes were just sparkling with curiosity. Finally one of the men said, "I think women are superior to men," to which there was a chorus of almost envious agreement from all the other men present. Surprised at this admission, I responded, "Really? In what way?" "Well," he said, "look at the things they can do with their bodies. They can have a baby and feed it, too. They're smarter. They handle crises better...." This guy had a list! And all of his peers were in agreement! This was a revelation for me. Contrary to popular belief, ladies, men have long been harboring secret admiration for us in their hearts. They may not be telling us about it, but it's there. (Isn't it something that they envy our childbearing abilities, and yet so many women have no appreciation for this unique gift?) They battle with feelings of inferiority and the fear of being all thumbs in our presence. Now, as you know, bad little boys will always cover up their fear by being bullies. But there is a world of nice men wandering around out there who simply don't know what to do. Our mission is to know a bully when we see one and not allow his fears to move us off our mark as a woman. Either disarm him with kindness or avoid him if he is abusive. As for the nice guys, we need to help them out by being nice back to them. They are the ones who prove to be worth the work in the long run.

The bottom line on this femininity thing? Women need men, women need one another, but most of all women need God. No matter what the issue, it all comes back—full circle—to Him. After all, we were really created for God's pleasure, first and foremost. He is pleased when we walk in the office of our femininity. It is in pleasing Him that we are pleased. You see, good worship is reciprocal.

> "Worthy art Thou, our Lord and our God, to receive
> glory and honor and power; for Thou didst create all
> things, and because of Thy will they existed and
> were created" (Revelation 4:11 NASB).

God is the secret to us maintaining our femininity—in the boardroom, on the street, in our homes, no matter where we are or what we come up against. God is our champion in every cause if we are submitted to Him. All we have to *do* is *be*. He will fight for our rights, be our protector, and advocate for us as we, like Mary, purpose to be servants of the Lord, wholly available and obedient to Him. So be free to be feminine. Rejoice in being everything you were created to be as a woman. Revel in it. Get downright excited about it. Celebrate your uniqueness. Embrace your softness. Cherish your tenderness. Delight in your warmth. Enjoy your laughter. Discover the beauty of your tears. No matter what size you are, appreciate every curve, every roll, every bump, every line. And then lift your eyes heavenward and worship the One who loves you most.

> "Grace and peace be multiplied to you in the knowl-
> edge of God and of Jesus our Lord; seeing that His
> divine power has granted to us everything pertaining
> to life and godliness, through the true knowledge of
> Him who called us by His own glory and excellence.
> For by these He has granted to us His precious and
> magnificent promises, in order that by them you
> might become partakers of the divine nature, having
> escaped the corruption that is in the world by lust.
> Now for this very reason also, applying all diligence,
> in your faith supply moral excellence, and in your
> moral excellence, knowledge, and in your knowl-

edge, self-control, and in your self-control, perseverance, and in your perseverance, godliness, and in
your godliness, [sisterly] kindness, and in your [sis-
terly] kindness, love. For if these qualities are yours
and are increasing, they render you neither useless
nor unfruitful in the true knowledge of our Lord
Jesus Christ" (2 Peter 1:2-8 NASB).

*Dear Heavenly Father, thank You. Thank You for creating me
just as I am—a complex and incredible woman. Forgive me for
the times I have allowed myself to forget who I am and why I
was created. Create in me the heart of a woman as You
ordained it to be. Restore to me the joy of my femininity. Impart
a spirit of excellence in me that I might be a force in my home,
in my church, in my community, and in my world. Help my
hands to always heal, my arms to always comfort, my spirit to
always nurture, my words to always edify, and my nature to
always serve. Let my presence always be an oasis for those who
gather in my shade. Teach me to render praise. Grant me the
heart of a true worshiper. Heal the broken places within me and
sever me from my past afflictions. Renew my mind and liberate
my soul to rise again in spite of all past hindrances. Instruct me
in the way of Your Word that I might be the woman, the sister,
the mother, the wife, and the influence You've called me to be.
Help me to remember at all times that all I do and all I say is
ultimately for Your glory. In Jesus' name. Amen.*

Recommended Reading

Fashioned for Intimacy
Jane Hansen, Regal Books

The Master's Degree
Frank and P.B. Wilson, Harvest House Publishers

Chosen Vessels
Rebecca Osaigbovo, Dabar Publishing

Opposites Attract
Tim and Beverly LaHaye, Harvest House Publishers

Liberated by Submission
P.B. Wilson, Harvest House Publishers

C.S. Lewis on Love
C.S. Lewis, Thomas Nelson Publishers

The Lady, Her Lover, and Her Lord
T.D. Jakes, Putnam

Fascinating Woman
Helen Andelin, Bantam Books

The Book of Romance
Tommy Nelson, Thomas Nelson Publishers

What Makes a Man Feel Loved
Bob Barnes, Harvest House Publishers

Woman Thou Art Loosed
T.D. Jakes, Albury Publishers

The Act of Marriage
Tim and Beverly LaHaye, Zondervan Publishers

Men and Women Enjoying the Difference
Dr. Larry Crabb, Zondervan Publishers

The Unique Woman
Edwin and Nancy Cole, Honor Books

Recovering Biblical Manhood and Womanhood
John Piper and Wayne Grudem, Crossway Books